A CONCISE GUIDE TO
CATS

A CONCISE GUIDE TO
CATS

Emily Williams

p

This is a Parragon Book
First published in 2006

Parragon
Queen Street House
4 Queen Street
Bath, BA1 1HE

Produced by Atlantic Publishing

See page 256 for
photograph copyright details
Text © Parragon Books Ltd 2006

ISBN 1 40547 331 2
Printed in China

CONTENTS

SHORTHAIR CATS 92–149

CATS WITH SPECIAL CHARACTERISTICS 150–187

CHOOSING AND CARING FOR YOUR CAT 188

KEEPING YOUR CAT HEALTHY 200

INTRODUCTION

T he cat is the most popular household pet across most of the countries in Europe and in much of North America, even though it is essentially an independent spirit. Left to its own devices a cat will survive quite well without any humans around, although it will replace human companionship with that of other cats because it is essentially a social animal. As well as its beautiful looks, it is this sense of being self-contained that appeals to many people and leads them to choose a cat to share their home, rather than any other kind of animal.

Cats have been enchanting us for thousands of years, and will no doubt continue to do so for thousands more to come. Sharing your life with a cat is a satisfying and enjoyable experience – you are not only taking on a friend for life but also gaining a unique opportunity to observe the natural world at close quarters. Our enjoyment of cats can only be enhanced by understanding them better, by looking at their history and behaviour and seeing how this may indicate their needs and wants.

From wild cats to household pets

The Cat Family as a whole includes both big cats, such as the Lion, Leopard and Tiger, and small cats, such as the Bobcat, Puma and Wildcat. The original distinction between these two was based not only on size, but also on sound – big cats roar, small cats purr. This is not just a matter of volume – small cats have a rigid hyoid bone connecting the tongue to the roof of the mouth, while in big cats it is flexible. Big cats cannot purr in the same way as small cats, even if they wanted to. Another difference between the two is that big cats generally feed lying down, while small cats stand up. However, there are also many similarities between the

two. When you see big cats in their natural habitat, it can often seem as if they are behaving like larger versions of the cat at home. Cubs roll around and play together just like kittens, the mother moves them around by the scruff of the neck, as a mother cat does, and a big cat basking in the sun can be very reminiscent of a household cat on a sunny lawn.

There are some areas of the world that do not have any kind of cat as part of their natural wildlife. Before felines developed, Australia and South America had separated from other parts of the land mass. Cats evolved in North America and Eurasia, and were able to cross into South America when it linked up with the northern continent, but there was no land bridge to Australia. Many smaller islands had no equivalent of the cat either – which often led to disaster amongst the local wildlife if a domestic pet was later introduced,

Although it may look like many other members of the Cat Family, the domestic cat is descended from the African Wildcat, which is one of the small cats. Unlike other domestic animals, such as the dog, the cat chose to become domesticated – it began to live in close proximity to human settlements as it quickly realized that they were a good source of food. Wall paintings from Ancient Egypt dating back to 4000 BC show cats as part of the agricultural scene – grain

Left: An ancient Egyptian depiction of a cat fighting a snake. The Egyptians associated the cat with fertility but also admired its agility and strength as a hunter.

storage attracted rats and so offered plenty of food for cats, while farmers no doubt appreciated the natural pest control. Evidence of cats living near people even earlier than this have been found in Israel, Cyprus and India. In Egypt, by around 1700 BC, cats had moved up to become domestic pets, rather than just vermin control.

Domestic cats were often taken on board ship by early traders and settlers because of their ability to control vermin, and in this way the domesticated cat spread to India by around 400 BC, and to southern Russia and northern Europe by AD 100. It did not arrive in the New World in any great numbers until the eighteenth century, when cats were specifically imported into the east to control rodents. These original immigrants soon multiplied and spread, until they were found across the continent.

Cats in religion and literature

Although cats originally may have been appreciated for their excellent hunting abilities, in Egypt by 1400 BC they had been raised to the status of a god. The cat was associated with Bast, the goddess of love and fertility, and anyone who killed a cat could be sentenced to death. Export of the sacred animal was forbidden, and families went into mourning if their cat died. Other religions have honoured cats, including Islam – because the Prophet Muhammad was very fond of them – and several Indian faiths that teach reverence for all living things. The cat has not done quite so well with Christians – it has often been associated with the devil or with witchcraft. Superstitions hold that cats can bring both good luck and bad – in Britain if a black cat crosses your path it was held to be lucky, in North America it was unlucky. In Japan, a cat with one paw held upright is a good luck symbol, while in Europe a cat with its paw behind its ear is supposed to foretell rain.

With all these beliefs surrounding it, it is not surprising that the cat has found a place in art and literature as well. Japanese art often features cats, both in paintings and made of ivory or bronze. In India, China and Thailand cats were highly regarded, and were often included in religious paintings, or to symbolize high status in pictures that told a story. In the west cats in paintings more usually symbolized evil or treachery until the 18th century, after which they began to appear in the role of beloved domestic pet. Stories featuring cats include several of Aesop's fables, which were written in around 500 BC, and the fairy tales Puss in

Boots and Dick Whittington, which both have a cat in a starring role. Several famous children's books are based on cats, including Kathleen Hale's series about Orlando, the marmalade cat and Dr Seuss' *The Cat in the Hat*.

In day to day life, as ordinary people began to have more leisure time, cats also moved on from mouser to pampered pet. It was not long before particular attributes came to be prized, which led to cats being exhibited at shows and eventually to the development of pedigree breeds. The first recorded cat show was in 1871 at Crystal Palace in London. In America too cat shows were being introduced and the Maine Coon was established as a popular breed. Interest grew, not only in breeding cats with longer hair and attractive colouring but also in more exotic breeding stock. By the end of the nineteenth century Siamese cats had been imported into Britain and during the first decade of the new century Siamese cat clubs were founded on both sides of the Atlantic. In Britain the Governing Council of the Cat Fancy was founded in 1910 to establish breed standards and look after the welfare of pedigree cats. Although at first dealing with just a few hundred cats, the association now registers over 30,000 pedigree cats each year. Similar organizations now exist all over the world in countries as diverse as Brazil and Estonia.

But although there are now thousands of pedigree cats, they are vastly outnumbered by the ordinary household moggie. Owning a cat is no longer a preserve of the rich – anyone can have one. It has been proved that people who own cats visit the doctor less often than those who don't, that stroking a cat lowers your blood pressure, and that people who suffer serious illnesses recover better if they have a pet cat. However, ownership of a cat – if it can be called that with such an independent creature – is not something to be taken on lightly. If you are planning to become a cat owner for the first time, make sure you understand the costs and commitment you are taking on, and make an effort to find the right cat to suit your lifestyle. If you get it right, you will not only gain an endless source of entertainment and comfort, but also a loyal companion.

DEVELOPMENT
OF THE
DOMESTIC CAT

THE CAT FAMILY

The cat family shares the same roots as other predator mammals and the family is divided into two species, Old World and New World. All animals have a Latin scientific name as well as their common name. The first part of this is known as the genus, and indicates a group within a family that is closely related; the second part distinguishes the particular animal. Most big cats, such as the Leopard and the Lion, are members of the genus Panthera, while small cats, such as the Bobcat and the African Wildcat, are members of the genus Felis. The division was originally made on the basis that cats that could roar were Panthera, and cats that could not were Felis, although in addition there are a couple of anomalies, such as the Cheetah, which belongs to the genus Acinonyx, and the Clouded Leopard, which belongs to the genus Neofelis. Unfortunately this neat arrangement has been challenged in recent years, since genetic fingerprinting has shown that cats on different continents are in fact closely related, and that cats that may look and behave very differently share the same DNA and therefore should belong to the same genus.

BIG CATS

The term Big Cats is used to cover the Tiger, Leopard, Lion, Jaguar, Cheetah and Clouded Leopard. Despite the difference in scale there are many similarities between them and domestic cats. Young are born in litters, blind and helpless, and are looked after by the mother until they are old enough to fend for themselves. Big cats are distributed across a wide area of the globe, but their numbers are declining due both to hunting and to loss of their natural habitat.

Tiger

The Tiger (*Panthera tigris*) is found across India, China, Siberia and Indonesia, but only in isolated groups. It prefers forested country, but also lives on rocky mountainsides. The adult lives alone, the male defending a large territory that may overlap the areas of several females, but tiger cubs stay with their mother until they are 2–3 years old. The Tiger's coat is striped in dark and light vertical bands, providing ideal camouflage as it hunts.

Leopard

The Leopard (*Panthera pardus*) is found across Africa to the Far East, in forests, grasslands and even desert areas. The adult lives alone, the male defending a large territory from other males, although it may overlap the territories of some females. The Leopard's coat is fawn with black spots arranged in rosettes, but there is also a natural variation with a completely black coat, which was once classified as a distinct species, the panther.

Lion

The Lion (*Panthera leo*) is found in Africa, with a few scattered in northern India, in grassland or scrub country – despite its nickname 'King of the Jungle', it does not live in forests. Lions are very sociable and live in prides of related females, along with one or two males, who stay only a few years and then move on. Cubs have spotted coats for camouflage, but the spotting fades considerably as they grow, and the adult has a beautiful golden ticked tabby coat.

Above: Like the domestic cat, the Cheetah uses its tongue to groom itself and keep its coat in good condition.
Opposite: The mother domestic cat carries her young by the scruff of the neck causing the kitten to stop struggling and draw in its legs. Big cats, for example this Lion, carry their cubs in the same manner.

Jaguar

The Jaguar (*Panthera onca*) is found in the tropical forests of South and Central America, usually near water. It is the New World equivalent of the Leopard, living alone on territory that it defends, and with a similar blotched and spotted coat. Although classified as Panthera, the Jaguar seldom roars.

Cheetah

The Cheetah (*Acinonyx jubatus*) is now quite rare, but was once found on grasslands across northern Africa, southern Asia and the Middle East. The Cheetah's claws are quite blunt, so it hunts by running after its prey — it is the fastest moving animal on earth in short bursts — then knocking it over and strangling it. Cubs have to be taught to hunt by their mother, as they are unable to learn the skill on their own. The Cheetah has quite distinct black spots on a fawn background.

Above: Testing of DNA has proved that the African Wildcat is the true ancestor of the domestic cat. Unlike other wildcats, the African can be quite tame if it is raised in captivity.

Clouded Leopard

The Clouded Leopard (*Neofelis nebulosa*) is found in the tropical forests of South-eastern Asia, and sometimes in less forested areas and swampland. It is an extremely good climber and hunts both in trees and on the ground. Its unusual and distinctive coat is pale yellow–brown, with large irregular markings on its sides that are dark brown round the edge and lighter in the middle, and dark spots on legs and tail. Although it looks like a big cat, it is unable to roar.

SMALL CATS

The term Small Cats covers a wide variety of species in the genus Felis, some of which are only found in the Americas, others only in Africa and Eurasia. Many of the small cats are very similar in both size and appearance to the domestic cat, but they are wild by nature and it is impossible to tame them. As with the big cats, the number of small cats is declining, due to hunting for their pelts and to loss of habitat. Most of the less rare species are covered here, but there are several other species that are either found only in very small areas, or are so rare that they may become extinct.

African Wildcat

The African Wildcat (*Felis silvestris lybica*) is found across most of Africa, except in the true desert of the Sahara and the central rainforest belt. This species is the true ancestor of the domestic cat, and can still be relatively tame if it is raised in captivity. It has a banded tabby coat, with reddish fur behind the ears.

Asian Leopard

The Asian Leopard Cat (*Felis prionailurus bengalensis*) is found in South-east Asia, from Mongolia through China and Indo-China to the East Indies. It is around the size of a domestic cat, but is too wild to make a good pet. However it has been bred with domestic cats to create the Bengal (see page 136).

Bobcat

The Bobcat (*Felis lynx rufus* or *Lynx rufus*) is found only in North America, where it is the most common wildcat. It prefers rocky, wooded terrain, often hiding during the day in rocky clefts. It is a subspecies of the Lynx, but is slightly larger, and gets its name from its stubby tail.

Chinese Desert Cat

The Chinese Desert Cat (*Felis bieti*) is found only in China, on steppes or in mountain brush or forest – it is not a desert-dweller, despite its name. It is closely related to the Wildcat, but has a yellow-brown coat with few markings except for a few slightly darker streaks on the legs and haunches and rings on the tail. It is slightly larger than a domestic cat, and has thick hair over its footpads, possibly to aid in walking on hot sand and cold snow.

European Wildcat

The European Wildcat (*Felis silvestris europeus*) is closely related to the Spanish Wildcat and the Scottish Wildcat, but is found in mainland Europe in isolated pockets, particularly in Germany, France, Spain, parts of eastern Europe and west of the Caspian Sea. It was once almost extinct, but is now protected in many areas.

It looks very like the African Wildcat, but is generally darker grey or brown in colour, and unlike the African species it is untameable.

Indian Desert Cat

The Indian Desert Cat (*Felis silvestris ornata*) is related to both the African and European Wildcats, but is found from Russia into India and southern Asia. It is smaller than the other two species, and has a coat that is spotted rather than striped. It has a light-coloured coat, more like the African Wildcat than the European, with more distinct markings than either.

Jungle Cat

The Jungle Cat (*Felis chaus*) is found in parts of Egypt, the Middle East, southern Asia and western China, usually on grassland or near forests, but always near water. It is sandy to red-brown or grey and the tip of the tail is black.

Lynx

The Lynx has a far wider range than other small cats, being found on both sides of the Atlantic. The Canadian Lynx (*Felis lynx canadensis* or *Lynx canadensis*) is found across most of Canada in forested areas, scrub and tundra; the European Lynx (*Felis lynx pardina* or *Lynx pardina*) is found in the forests of northern Europe, and the Eurasian Lynx (*Felis lynx lynx* or *Lynx lynx*) is found in Siberian forests. The Lynx has a spotted coat, but the Canadian Lynx's spots are less defined than the other species.

Ocelot

The Ocelot (*Felis pardalis* or *Leopardus pardalis*) is found in Central America and the northern countries of South America, except for Chile. It has been hunted to extinction in many areas for its beautiful coat, which is yellow-cream with dark brown irregular spots, rosettes and stripes, edged in black.

Opposite: The African Serval can grow to around one metre in length.

Puma

The Puma (*Felis concolor* or *Puma concolor*) is also sometimes known as the Cougar, Florida Panther, Red Tiger or Mountain Lion. It inhabits both North and South America, but in many areas has been hunted almost to extinction because of its preference for eating domestic livestock. It has grey-brown fur on the upper body, with creamy white on the chest and stomach.

Sand Cat

The Sand Cat (*Felis margarita*) is found only in desert areas of North Africa, Arabia, Central Asia and Pakistan. It has a pale grey to sandy yellow coat with a few indistinct slightly darker stripes, and more distinct bands on the legs. It is the smallest of the wildcats, and has thick hair over its footpads to aid in walking on hot sand.

Scottish Wildcat

The Scottish Wildcat (*Felis silvestris grampia*) is closely related to the European Wildcat, but is found only in the Scottish highlands. It looks very like the African Wildcat, but is generally darker grey or brown in colour, and unlike the African species it is untameable. It has a broader head than the domestic cat – most wildcat species have larger brains, due to the demands of survival in the wild.

Spanish Wildcat

The Spanish Wildcat (*Felis silvestris iberia*) is closely related to the European Wildcat, but is found only in isolated areas of Iberia. It looks very like a domestic tabby, but is untameable. Wildcats were found across the Old World, but as they became isolated they developed in slightly different ways and were divided down to be classed as subspecies.

DOMESTIC CATS

Investigation has proved that the African Wildcat, which was first domesticated in ancient Egypt, is the ancestor of all domestic cats. Genetically, all domestic cats are tabbies because the African Wildcat has a coat with bands of lighter and darker colours like a striped tabby, designed to provide camouflage in the wild. Therefore, although all cats still carry the tabby gene, mutated genes can mask it so that the coat appears in another pattern or colour.

Mutations leading to single colours or different patterns have always occurred naturally, but in the domestic cat they did not die out as they would in the wild, because a household pet does not need camouflage to survive. After cats became pets, nature created hundreds of different coat patterns, colours and textures without any help from humans at all. In addition cats responded to environmental conditions – those living in cold climates developed thicker coats, those hunting bigger prey grew larger – and a whole range of different permutations were established. A non-pedigree cat is actually a walking feline gene pool, from which breeders can select the traits they want. Over hundreds of years, breeders have worked with these naturally occurring variations, accentuating and refining selected traits to create pedigree or purebred cats in established colours and patterns.

COLOURS, PATTERNS AND SHAPES

COLOURS

There are basically eight coat colours, four deep and four dilute, plus White, although breed associations confuse matters by giving the same colour different names for different breeds. When the colour is distributed evenly along the length of the hair, it appears denser – these deep colours are Black, Red, Chocolate and Cinnamon. If the colour is patchy and uneven along the hair the colour is lighter – these dilute colours are Blue, Cream, Lilac or Lavender, and Fawn.

A White coat (*opposite*) is caused by a dominant gene that masks all the other colours, but it is also associated with deafness. Eighty-five per cent of white cats with blue eyes are deaf.

Black (*below*) is the most common solid colour, as the gene for Black masks those for all the other colours except White or Red.

The colour that breeders call Red (*above*) is really more a deep orange and is a traditional colour in Western breeds. Cream (*below*) is the dilute version of Red.

Chocolate (*above*), a dark brown, is a traditional colour in Eastern cats, but has now been bred into many Western breeds.

Cinnamon (*below*) is also an Eastern colour – it is a lighter brown than Chocolate.

Blue (*above*) is really more a blue-grey and is the dilute version of Black. Fawn (*below*) is the dilute version of Cinnamon. Lilac or Lavender (*opposite*) is the dilute version of Chocolate.

PATTERNS

T he hair in the lighter areas of a tabby coat is not just one paler colour – it has bands of colour along its length, usually light at the base and darker towards the tip. This creates a speckled effect that, combined with the pattern of darker stripes and spots, helps the cat to blend into its background. These banded hairs are called agouti hairs, after a rodent that has the same kind of striped hair. 'Agouti' is also used to describe the paler areas of a tabby coat in general. The darker hairs making up the stripes and spots of a tabby have no banding, so they are non-agouti hairs. Opposing the gene causing agouti hairs there is a non-agouti gene that masks it; there is also a range of genes causing different colour effects, which combine in different ways to create a range of coat patterns.

Solid or Self

Cats that appear to be one solid colour have mostly non-agouti hairs in their coat. Even these cats carry the tabby gene, so it may be possible to see faint tabby markings – or ghost markings – in a bright light.

Opposite: This Silver Tabby is a fine example of the classic tabby pattern.

Tabby

There are four different types of tabby pattern – classic, mackerel, spotted and ticked.

Classic tabbies have broad swirls or circles on their sides, around a central blotch.

Mackerel tabbies have narrow parallel dark streaks running downwards from the spine like a fish skeleton. They are also sometimes called tiger cats.

Spotted tabbies are quite rare, but have breaks in the dark stripes of the mackerel or classic tabby pattern, creating spots.

Ticked tabbies have coats made up almost entirely of agouti hairs, so they have a subtle speckled pattern with striping only on the head, and sometimes the legs and tail.

Silver Tabby

The silver gene can lighten the agouti hairs and mask the yellow-tan colour, turning the cat into Silver Tabby.

Opposite: This chinchilla's undercoat is white but the tips of the hairs are darker.
Above: In the pointed coat pattern the hairs on the coolest points of the body have extra colour.
Below: This Burmilla is Brown shaded with Silver.

Above: Cats with large areas of white on their bodies are known as Piebald. The coloured areas can be any colour or pattern.

Smoke

In cats with a solid colour coat the silver gene makes the base of the hair lighter or whiter, creating a shimmering undercoat when the cat moves.

Shaded

Shaded coats have mostly agouti hairs, which have wide light-coloured bands and narrow dark-coloured bands, creating a subtle shaded ticked pattern.

Tipped or Chinchilla

These are coats in which most of the hair is white and only the tip is coloured.

Pointed

In pointed coats, which are mostly associated with Siamese cats, the pigment in the hair is heat sensitive. The fur on the body is pale, but the hair on the cooler extremities or 'points' – the ears, nose, feet and tail – is darker.

> Colourpoint cats have points in a solid colour. They are usually described by colour, so a cat with Chocolate pointing will be described as a Chocolate Point.
>
> Tortie Point cats have tortoiseshell patterning in the darker areas.
>
> Tabby or Lynx Point cats have tabby stripes in the darker areas.

Piebald

Bi-colour cats have large areas of white combined with patches of colour, usually on their heads and bodies.

Van

Van cats are mostly white with patches of colour mainly on heads and tails.

Tortoiseshell

Tortoiseshell coats are typically red and black, and they are almost invariably found on the female because the gene that determines red hair is carried on the X chromosome. If this gene is dominant it makes the coat red; if it is recessive the coat can be any other colour, but will most likely be black as this masks other colours. Male cats are XY – i.e. they only have one X chromosome and therefore one copy of the red gene, so the coat can be red or black but not both. Female cats are XX, so they can have two copies of the red gene, and if one is dominant and one recessive they can have both red and black colouring in their coats. Tortoiseshell patterns can also be in the dilute colours of Blue and Cream.

Calico

This coat is essentially a tortoiseshell with large patches of white. It is supposed to be named after calico cloth.

SHAPE AND FORM

S ince most colours and patterns are common to all breeds, the different breeds are also defined by build, head and eye shape, coat length and special characteristics. Some of these differences were originally due to natural variation, others to environmental factors, but breeders have selected traits and developed them to create new breeds.

Build

The range of body types in a cat goes from one extreme to the other. At one end of the spectrum it is short, compact and heavy-boned – known as cobby – at the other, long-legged, lithe and fine-boned – called Oriental. In between is an average build, which covers most cats. These body types have not come about accidentally – they originally evolved in response to local conditions, so they indicate to some extent which part of the world the breed's natural ancestors come from. The heavier, stockier breeds tend to be those descended from cats from northern areas, which had to cope with cold climates – they are built to conserve body heat. At the other extreme, very slender cats with long bodies evolved in hot climates – they needed to lose body heat, not retain it, and their body shape gives them the maximum surface area to do this. Over time breeders have changed the look of some breeds quite considerably, making some more 'Oriental' and others rounder and stockier than they originally were.

Opposite top: This Manx cat is a good example of the compact, heavy, cobby body type.
Opposite below: Most domestic shorthairs, such as this Spotted Tabby, have an intermediate body shape.
Overleaf: Oriental cats typically have a long, lean body that is quite tubular.

Head

The head of a cat can be round, rectangular or wedge-shaped, or a range of shapes in between. Oriental cats typically have wedge-shaped or triangular heads. This is another trait that has been worked on by breeders, sometimes with unfortunate results for the cats' health. For instance, breeding for large heads in the Persian has meant that a Caesarean delivery of the kittens is often required.

Below: The head of the Bengal is quite rounded in shape.
Opposite: The European Burmese has the typical wedge-shaped head of Oriental breeds.

Eyes

The eyes of cats are quite large in relation to the size of their head and body, which is one of their most appealing characteristics. Wild cats usually have copper eyes, although they are sometimes more green or yellow, but domestic cats have a range of eye colours. The eye colour is not normally genetically related to the colour of the coat, but breed standards sometimes state an ideal eye colour to go with a specific coat colour, so the breeder will select with this in mind. The only exception to this is blue eyes, which are normally caused by the gene that also masks the colours of the coat, so blue-eyed cats usually have coats with a great deal of white. Unfortunately this gene is also related to deafness, which is why blue-eyed cats are often deaf. The blue eyes in Siamese cats are caused by a different gene, and there may also be other rare genes causing blue eyes that are as yet unresearched.

Below: The Snow Bengal has blue eyes and a pale coat.
Opposite: This Sphynx has one blue and one green-gold eye, a trait that can be quite common in some breeds, such as the Turkish Van.

COAT LENGTH

T he African Wildcat has a short, fine coat, and a shorthaired coat is therefore the natural length for the domestic cat. However, the type and length of a coat that is classed as shorthaired may vary considerably from breed to breed. The Siamese has a thin, sparse coat that lies close to its body, but the Exotic Shorthair has a thick, plush double coat that stands out from the body and looks twice as long.

The gene that causes long hair was almost certainly originally a natural mutation. Although the longhair gene is recessive, natural selection in colder climates favoured cats with longer, thicker coats, so in some breeds it became the norm. However, longhaired kittens were occasionally born in the litters of normally shorthaired breeds, and in some cases they have been developed into a separate breed. For instance, the Somali is the longhaired version of the Abyssinian, and the Scottish Fold is the longhaired version of the Highland Fold.

Wavy or curled hair, known as a rex coat, are also caused by a gene mutation that occurs spontaneously. In the wild such cats would soon die out, but in domestic breeds this trait can be preserved

Opposite: This lovely Cinnamon Angora gets its colour from its Abyssinian parentage, and the long coat from a dormant longhair gene.

with breeding programmes. In both the Cornish Rex and the Devon Rex the gene is recessive, so some inbreeding is needed to preserve the curled coat. However, rexed coats are not all caused by the same gene, so crossing the Cornish Rex and the Devon Rex gives straight-haired kittens. In the Selkirk Rex the rex gene is dominant, so even outcrossing to other breeds will produce a percentage of kittens with rexed coats.

Another, even more unusual, coat mutation is hairlessness, such as in the Sphynx and the Peterbald. Hairless cats have appeared at various times across the world, but again such animals would quickly die out in the wild because they have no protection from heat or cold. The Sphynx is the most successful of the hairless breeds, but it is still not clear if the gene that causes the lack of coat will also lead to any ongoing health problems.

Left: The majority of cats are short-haired and need very little grooming.

Special Characteristics

Some breeds are instantly recognizable without looking at their colour, shape or coat length. They have unique defining characteristics, such as the folded ears of the Scottish Fold or the curled ears of the American Curl, and the lack of tail in the

Above: Although it appears hairless the Sphynx is covered in fine down, but this offers little protection against heat and cold.
Opposite: The American Curl is a relatively new breed that was developed in the 1980s.

Manx. These traits are all caused by mutated genes but have been retained with controlled breeding programmes. Some of these breeds are not recognized by some of the main registries, as mutations such as these often also cause unpleasant side effects that are bad for the health of the cat. The gene for folded ears in the Scottish Fold can also cause abnormal bone growth in adult cats, and the Manx is prone to kittens dying soon after birth, or fatal bowel or bladder problems.

CAT BREEDS:

Only a very small number of all the cats in the world can claim to have a pedigree but the classification of pedigree cats is a complex business. The same breed can have different names depending on what part of the world it comes from, and what are recognized as distinct breeds in some countries are only considered to be colour variants in others. The various associations each produce their own breed standards by which cats are judged in competition.

The following sections divide cats into three groups: longhair cats, shorthair cats and cats with recognizable characteristics, regardless of the length of coat, such as folded or curled ears, rex coats or bob-tails.

BREEDS:
LONGHAIR AND
SEMI-LONGHAIR CATS

PERSIAN

The typical snub nose, large round head and compact body of the Persian is well known around the world – 75 per cent of registered pedigree cats are Persians. Longhaired cats were first imported into Italy from Persia in the 1620s, and their descendants were known by a variety of names. The Persian breed was developed in the late 1800s, but cats today look significantly different, with broader, flatter faces. This is a quiet, gentle but inquisitive cat, very placid and happy to be around children in family life, or to be a contented lap cat. Its long, silky thick fur needs daily grooming to remove loose hair and keep it looking its best, and regular baths are also a good idea. There are more than fifty coat colours and patterns, so almost every type is represented (a small selection of these is shown overleaf). Some registries designate the different colours as different breeds and a shorthaired version has also now been developed, the Exotic Shorthair.

ALTERNATIVE NAMES: Longhair; Turkish Angora; Kashmir
ORIGIN: United Kingdom
WEIGHT: 3.5–6.25 kg (8–14 lbs)
DESCRIPTION: Muscular, compact-bodied cat, with a large round head, small, round tipped ears set low, large, round widely spaced eyes, short, thick legs and a fairly short but very full tail. The long, thick and silky coat is very soft and luxuriant
GROOMING: Daily grooming required
TEMPERAMENT: Quiet, placid
SIMILAR BREEDS: None

Opposite Above: Chocolate Persian Tabby kitten
Opposite Below: Golden Shaded Persian cat
Above: Red and White Persian cat

COLOURPOINT LONGHAIR OR HIMALAYAN

This breed is essentially a Persian cat, but has the Siamese pointed pattern. It is known as Colourpoint Longhair in many areas of the world, but usually as Himalayan in North America. It has the typical Persian snub nose, rounded head, stocky body and long, thick, silky coat with a majestic neck ruff. The body fur usually ranges from white to beige, with contrast pointing in a range of colours, either solid or in tortoiseshell or tabby pattern. This is a relaxed and sociable cat, happy with children and with the company of other animals. It is not particularly vocal, but its long, thick coat requires daily grooming to keep it in top condition. White cats will also need regular baths to keep them clean.

ALTERNATIVE NAMES: Himalayan; Colourpoint Persian

ORIGIN: United Kingdom and United States

WEIGHT: 4–6.75 kg (9–15 lbs)

DESCRIPTION: Medium to large, compact cat, with a round head, snub nose and full cheeks, small rounded ears, short strong legs and a short bushy tail. The large round eyes are bright blue and the coat is long, thick and silky

GROOMING: Daily grooming required

TEMPERAMENT: Docile, gentle, friendly

SIMILAR BREEDS: Colourpoint Longhair is a member of the Persian family, the other members of which look identical but have a wider range of coat colours. In North America, it is known as Himalayan

ANGORA

This breed was developed in Britain, and originates from breeding a Sorrel Abyssinian with a Seal Point Siamese. As well as other characteristics, the descendants inherited the gene for long hair, which led eventually to the Angora. The breed suffers from considerable confusion in its name, being known as the Javanese in Europe and previously called the Oriental Longhair in the United States — although this name now refers to an entirely different US breed. The Angora is not related to the Turkish Angora. It is an elegant and attractive cat, both inquisitive and lively, and very vocal. Its coat is medium-length and silky with little undercoat, so it is easy to groom.

ALTERNATIVE NAMES: Javanese, Oriental Longhair, Mandarin
ORIGIN: United Kingdom
WEIGHT: 3–5 kg (7–11 lbs)
DESCRIPTION: Medium-size, svelte, muscular cat, with a triangular wedge-shaped head, large pointed ears, long slender legs and a long tapering plumed tail. The almond-shaped eyes are green except for cats with a white coat, which have blue eyes
GROOMING: Little required
TEMPERAMENT: Attention-seeking, playful, energetic
SIMILAR BREEDS: In the US this breed was once known as Oriental Longhair, although there is now a separate US breed with this name. In mainland Europe the Angora is known as Javanese. In the US, Javanese is used for selected colours of Balinese. Turkish Angora is a different breed

BIRMAN

This striking cat is supposed to have descended from the temple cats of Burma. According to legend, a pure white cat was one of the sacred companions of a golden goddess with blue eyes. When her temple was attacked, the cat's fur became tinged with gold and its eyes turned blue, inspiring the monks to rise up and protect the goddess. The other temple cats also took on these colours, and the Birman is said to be descended from one of them, crossed with a Persian or Siamese. Alternatively, a few people believe that the Birman was created by French breeders, but this theory is not very popular. It is a large, placid cat, very happy with children, self-contained and quiet. The coat is long and silky, and the classic colour is Seal Point, although there is a range of other colours. The feet have white mittens.

ALTERNATIVE NAMES: Sacred Cat of Burma; Tibetan Temple Cat
ORIGIN: Myanmar (formerly Burma)
WEIGHT: 3.5–8 kg (8–18 lbs)
DESCRIPTION: Large, stocky, powerfully built cat, with a broad rounded head, medium-size, well-spaced ears, vivid blue eyes, medium-length thick-set legs and full, fluffy tail. The coat is medium-long and silky
GROOMING: Daily grooming required
TEMPERAMENT: Placid, playful
SIMILAR BREEDS: Ragdoll generally has a deeper body colour and gauntlets that extend over the hock

BALINESE

The Balinese is essentially a longhaired Siamese. Siamese cats occasionally produced longhaired kittens but authorities are divided on whether these were the result of a spontaneous mutation, a previously masked longhaired gene, or a Siamese-Angora or Siamese-Persian outcross. Eventually a proper breeding programme was begun to create a longhaired Siamese, which was christened Balinese after the graceful temple dancers of Bali. The coat is only medium-length, but the plumed tail is quite distinctive. In Europe, all coat colours in this breed are classed as Balinese, but in North America only Seal, Blue, Chocolate and Lilac Points are Balinese, other colours being classed as Javanese.

ALTERNATIVE NAMES: Javanese
ORIGIN: United States
WEIGHT: 2.75–4.5 kg (6–10 lbs)
DESCRIPTION: Medium-size, slim, graceful cat, with a long wedge-shaped head, large pointed ears, blue almond-shaped eyes, slender legs and a long plumed tail. The coat is medium-long, fine and silky
GROOMING: Little required
TEMPERAMENT: Demanding, affectionate, playful, energetic
SIMILAR BREEDS: US Javanese is identical to the Balinese but has tabby, tortie or flame points

ORIENTAL LONGHAIR

The name Oriental Longhair was previously used for the Angora in North America, but this was misleading as it implied that the Angora was a longhaired Oriental Shorthair, when in fact it is not related to this breed at all. Now the Oriental Longhair correctly designates a longhaired Oriental without pointing, a breed that came about from the mating of an Oriental Shorthair and a Balinese. Longhaired Orientals with pointing are either classed as Balinese or Javanese. The Oriental Longhair is an inquisitive, energetic and friendly cat, happy to play with children, craving human company and often very vocal. Their long, silky hair lies flat against the body, so they can look very like Oriental Shorthairs except for their plumed tail.

ALTERNATIVE NAMES: Mandarin; Foreign Longhair
ORIGIN: North America
WEIGHT: 3.5–5.5 kg (8–12 lbs)
DESCRIPTION: Long, lean, sleek cat, with a long wedge-shaped head, large pointed ears, almond-shaped, slanted eyes, long slender legs and a plumed, gently tapering tail. The silky coat is semi-long, but lies flat to the body
GROOMING: Little required
TEMPERAMENT: Energetic, cuddly, inquisitive
SIMILAR BREEDS: The name Oriental Longhair was previously used in the US for the Angora, but this is a separate breed. Oriental Shorthair has a shorter coat, and the tail is not plumed

JAVANESE (US)

In the United States, the Javanese is essentially a longhaired colourpoint Siamese but in other colours than the traditional Seal, Blue, Chocolate or Lilac points. Authorities are divided on whether the occasional longhaired Siamese kittens that appeared in the past were the result of a spontaneous mutation, a previously masked longhaired gene, or a Siamese-Angora or Siamese-Persian outcross. A proper breeding programme created a longhaired Siamese, which was christened Balinese after the graceful temple dancers of Bali. The coat is only medium-length, but the plumed tail is quite distinctive. In Europe, all coat colours in this breed are classed as Balinese, and Javanese is used for the Angora.

ALTERNATIVE NAMES: Balinese
ORIGIN: United States
WEIGHT: 2.75–4.5 kg (6–10 lbs)
DESCRIPTION: Medium-size, slim, graceful cat, with a long wedge-shaped head, large pointed ears, blue almond-shaped eyes, slender legs and a long plumed tail. The coat is medium-long, fine and silky
GROOMING: Little required
TEMPERAMENT: Demanding, affectionate, playful, energetic
SIMILAR BREEDS: Balinese is identical to the US Javanese but has Seal, Blue, Chocolate or Lilac points

RAGDOLL

The Ragdoll gets its unusual name from its willingness to relax and go limp like a rag doll when picked up. It has an extremely easy-going, placid temperament and is affectionate, playful and sociable. It is also an extremely large and heavy cat, which reaches its full size and weight at around four years, with a semi-long, silky coat. This comes in only four colours – the classic pointed ones of Seal, Chocolate, Blue and Lilac – but also in three different patterns, as mitted and bi-colour are available as well as colourpoint. Authorities disagree on the breed's history – some hold that the breed is the result of a Persian-Birman cross, others that a non-pedigree longhair mated with a Birman, or that a feral cat mated with a Persian.

ALTERNATIVE NAMES: Original Ragdoll; Genuine Ragdoll; Cherubim Cat; Miracle Ragdoll
ORIGIN: United States
WEIGHT: 4.5–8 kg (10–18 lbs)
DESCRIPTION: Long, muscular cat, with a broad chest, rounded triangular head, large, oval blue eyes, medium ears with rounded tips, long legs and a long bushy tail. The coat is semi-long, densely soft and silky
GROOMING: Moderate grooming required
TEMPERAMENT: Placid, relaxed, sociable
SIMILAR BREEDS: Birman generally has a lighter body colour and gauntlets that stop at the hock

SOMALI

The forebears of the Abyssinian were probably brought to Britain by troops returning from the Abyssinian War in the late 1800s, although some authorities have alternative theories. Longhaired kittens occasionally appeared in litters and in the 1960s breeders began to establish a separate longhaired breed. Like the Abyssinian, this breed's most striking feature is the beautiful ticked pattern on its tabby coat, which appears to shimmer when the cat moves. The most common colour is a deep red brown, known as Ruddy in the US and Usual in the UK, but other colours include Red (Sorrel), Blue, Fawn and Silver. In summer the cat often loses much of its coat and can look shorthaired except for its plumed tail. The Somali is a sociable cat, happy around people and other animals, but likes its freedom and will not be happy if confined.

ALTERNATIVE NAMES: Longhaired Abyssinian
ORIGIN: North America
WEIGHT: 3.5–5 kg (8–11 lbs)
DESCRIPTION: Lithe, muscular cat, with rounded wedge-shaped head, large cupped and tufted ears, long slender legs, a medium-long soft coat, and a long, bushy tail. The rounded, almond-shaped eyes are gold or green
GROOMING: Moderate grooming required
TEMPERAMENT: Freedom-loving, active, sociable
SIMILAR BREEDS: Abyssinian has a more wedge-shaped head, shorter hair and does not have a plumed tail

TIFFANIE

This breed should not be confused with the Tiffany, which is the original name of what is now called Chantilly, an entirely separate breed. The Tiffanie is an Asian Longhair, descended from a Chinchilla Longhair-Burmese cross. In general body shape it is Burmese, but with the luxurious Chinchilla long coat. Its temperament is a good mixture of the two breeds – it is easy-going and lively, but not too boisterous, a gregarious cat that likes to play and to be in human company. The fine, silky coat does require regular grooming to keep it in good condition, but otherwise the Tiffanie is easy to care for. It comes in a wide range of self colours, as well as some shaded and tabby.

ALTERNATIVE NAMES: Asian Longhair
ORIGIN: United Kingdom
WEIGHT: 9–16 lbs (4–7.25 kg)
DESCRIPTION: Medium-size, well-muscled cat, with a short wedge-shaped head, large ears continuing the line of the face, medium legs and a long plumed tail. The rounded almond eyes are yellow to green and the semi-long coat is soft and silky
GROOMING: Moderate grooming required
TEMPERAMENT: Easy-going, affectionate, lively
SIMILAR BREEDS: None

TURKISH ANGORA

The Turkish Angora is an ancient and traditional breed that should not be confused with the British Angora, which is an entirely separate breed. The Turkish Angora developed naturally in Turkey, where it has been known for over 600 years. Although examples eventually found their way to France and Britain, it was not until the 1850s that the breed was distinguished from other longhaired cats. Due to cross-breeding with other longhairs the breed then more or less died out outside Turkey, but was re-established from Turkish stocks in the early 1950s. The Angora's glossy coat is not prone to matting, so requires only moderate grooming. All-white Angoras with blue eyes are prone to deafness, but there is a range of other coat colours as well as patterns such as tortoiseshell, tabby and bi-colour. Although loyal and loving, these cats are also energetic, playful and busy.

ALTERNATIVE NAMES: Ankhara; Angola
ORIGIN: Turkey
WEIGHT: 2.75–4.5 kg (6–10 lbs)
DESCRIPTION: Slender but well-muscled cat, with a small, rather wedge-shaped head, large oval eyes, large pointed ears set high, long legs with the hindlegs longer than the forelegs, and a plumed tail. The coat is long, fine and silky but has little undercoat
GROOMING: Moderate grooming required
TEMPERAMENT: Energetic, graceful, playful
SIMILAR BREEDS: Turkish Van has a heavier coat and bigger paws. Angora (Britain) or Javanese (Europe) is a different breed

TURKISH VAN

Unusually for a cat, the Turkish Van is famous for its love of water – in its homeland it is known as the 'swimming cat' and it will both swim and just lie in the water. Superficially similar to the Turkish Angora, the Van has a heavier coat and larger feet. The Turkish Van developed naturally in Turkey, but after kittens were imported to the West a breeding programme began. The favoured colour is white with coloured markings on the head and a coloured tail, with eyes either amber or blue – in Turkey the true Van is considered to be an all-white cat with odd eyes, but the breed is very rare there now. This is an intelligent, energetic cat, affectionate and quite self-contained, so it does not require constant attention.

ALTERNATIVE NAMES: Kurdish Van; Turkish Swimming Cat; White Ringtail
ORIGIN: Turkey
WEIGHT: 3–7.75 kg (7–17 lbs)
DESCRIPTION: Large, sturdy cat, with a short wedge-shaped head, oval eyes, large ears set close together high on the head, medium legs and a plumed tail. The coat is long, thick and silky
GROOMING: Moderate grooming required
TEMPERAMENT: Independent, intelligent, affectionate
SIMILAR BREEDS: Turkish Angora has a lighter coat and smaller feet

MAINE COON

Despite its long, luxurious coat, the Maine Coon is not a pampered lap cat. It is big and sturdily built, self-contained and an excellent hunter, much prized by farmers. It makes a great companion and is tolerant of children and other animals. Its exact origins are unknown – some accounts have it descended from Angoras sent to the US from France, others hold that its ancestors were Norwegian Forest Cats brought to North America by the Vikings. Its thick, glossy coat is water-resistant and excellent protection during the long cold winters in Maine, but needs grooming regularly to prevent it matting. Most coat colours and patterns are represented, but the classic Maine Coon is a tabby – traditionally in Brown.

ALTERNATIVE NAMES: American Forest Cat Longhair; American Longhair; American Shag; American Snughead; Maine Shag

ORIGIN: United States

WEIGHT: 4.5–9 kg (10–20 lbs)

DESCRIPTION: Large, solid, broad-chested cat, with a long body, large, upright pointed ears set high on the head, round eyes set slightly oblique, and a long, plumed tail. The coat is heavy, long and glossy

GROOMING: Moderate grooming required

TEMPERAMENT: Gentle, playful

SIMILAR BREEDS: Siberian has a more rounded body shape. Norwegian Forest Cat has almond-shaped eyes and rounded ears

NORWEGIAN FOREST CAT

The origins of the Norwegian Forest Cat are not entirely clear, but it is known that the Vikings established trade routes with Turkey, and Norwegian cats show some coat colours that are common in Turkey but rare elsewhere. The Turkish Angora could certainly have given the Norwegian cat its longhaired coat. Others believe that the Norwegian is descended from the Siberian in nearby Russia, which also has a dense, long coat. The Norwegian Forest Cat is a large, sturdy animal, with a water-repellent coat designed to withstand long, cold winters. It is a good climber and hunter, but loves to be around people and is good with children and other household pets. Outdoor cats shed their woolly undercoat in spring, at which point they need plenty of grooming to remove loose hairs. The coat comes in a wide range of colours and patterns.

ALTERNATIVE NAMES: Norsk Skaukatt; Skogkatt; Wegie
ORIGIN: Norway
WEIGHT: 3.5–8 kg (8–18 lbs)
DESCRIPTION: Large, sturdy, solid cat, with a triangular head, widely spaced ears set high, large almond-shaped eyes set obliquely, long sturdy legs and long bushy tail the same length as the body. The long coat is smooth, glossy and water-repellent, with a thick undercoat
GROOMING: Moderate grooming required
TEMPERAMENT: Gentle, friendly, reserved
SIMILAR BREEDS: Siberian has a more rounded body shape. Maine Coon has round eyes and pointed ears

SIBERIAN

The Siberian, or Siberian Forest Cat, is a large, sturdily built cat with a long coat — like the similar Norwegian Forest Cat and Maine Coon, it has developed this coat in response to harsh winter conditions. The coat is double, with a dense insulating undercoat and a thick waterproof topcoat. Brown Tabby is the most common colour, but a wide range of other tabby and some self and tortie colours are also found, particularly among cats bred in America. Russian breeders are intent on keeping the cat's original wild look and only accept brown and red-based coat colours. The Siberian developed from household and farm cats and was more or less unknown outside Russia until the 1980s, when the breed was first registered in St Petersburg. It is now recognized around the world, although cats bred in the West are beginning to look different from their Russian cousins.

ALTERNATIVE NAMES: Siberian Forest Cat
ORIGIN: Russia
WEIGHT: 5.5–9 kg (12–20 lbs)
DESCRIPTION: Large, powerful, well-muscled cat, with a broad head, large, oval, slightly slanted eyes, rounded ears angled outwards, muscular legs and a plumed tail with a rounded tip. The dense undercoat is covered by a long, thick topcoat, with a longer neck ruff
GROOMING: Moderate grooming required
TEMPERAMENT: Friendly, agile, loyal
SIMILAR BREEDS: Norwegian Forest Cat has a more rectangular body shape. Maine Coon also has a rectangular body shape and more pointed ears

BREEDS: SHORTHAIR CATS

EXOTIC SHORTHAIR

This breed is the shorthaired version of the longhaired Persian and shares many of its characteristics. It has the typical Persian snub nose, large round head and compact body with a short tail. It is a quiet, gentle but inquisitive cat, happy with children in family life and as a contented lap cat. The Exotic Shorthair does not have a really short coat – its fur is medium-length and very thick, and since it is a double coat it needs regular grooming to remove loose hair and keep it looking its best. The thickness of the coat makes the cat look very cuddly. There are over 100 coat colours and patterns, so almost every type is represented. The breed is still fairly uncommon, and longhaired kittens appear regularly in the litter.

ALTERNATIVE NAMES: Shorthair Persian
ORIGIN: United States
WEIGHT: 3.5–6 kg (8–13 lbs)
DESCRIPTION: Medium to large, short-bodied compact cat, with a rounded head, full cheeks and a snub nose, small wide-set ears, short, thick legs and a short tail. The round eyes are large and prominent and the coat is dense and plush
GROOMING: Moderate grooming required
TEMPERAMENT: Quiet, gentle, inquisitive
SIMILAR BREEDS: Persian is identical but has longer hair

AMERICAN SHORTHAIR

The domestic cats that arrived in North America with the first settlers from Europe adapted to local conditions over time, developing thick, dense coats and growing larger than their European cousins. The American Shorthair has been preserved as a breed since the early 1900s and is common in North America but less well known elsewhere. It was originally called the Domestic Shorthair, but many North American non-pedigree domestic cats share its characteristics, so the name was changed to differentiate the breed in the 1960s. Although the American Shorthair can have a coat in any colour or pattern, the classic tabby in Silver, Brown or Red is the most common. It is a sociable cat, happy with other animals and with children.

ALTERNATIVE NAMES: Domestic Shorthair
ORIGIN: United States
WEIGHT: 4–6.75 kg (9–15 lbs)
DESCRIPTION: Medium-size cat, with a wide, rounded face, large round eyes, wide-spaced ears rounded at the tip, muscular legs and a thick, medium-length tail. The coat is short, thick and very dense
GROOMING: Moderate grooming required
TEMPERAMENT: Intelligent, easy-going, sociable
SIMILAR BREEDS: British Shorthair is a more rounded, stocky cat; European Shorthair has a more triangular head with a well-defined muzzle

CALIFORNIA SPANGLED CAT

Although the California Spangled Cat may look as if it is descended from a wildcat, it is bred from a mixture of domestic cats, including pedigree breeds and a feral cat from Cairo. 'Spangled' is a term meaning 'spotted' in ornithology. The spotted tabby pattern of the coat of the California Spangled is similar to that of a leopard, with spotting on back and sides and stripes on top of the head and down the neck. The fur is short, but with longer hair on the tail and underbelly. This is a sweet-natured, undemanding cat, but quite self-contained and energetic. Although it has been around for some thirty years, this breed is still fairly uncommon, both in North America and in the rest of the world.

ALTERNATIVE NAMES: None
ORIGIN: United States
WEIGHT: 5.5–8 kg (12–18 lbs)
DESCRIPTION: Large, lean, long, well-muscled cat, with a rounded forehead, broad high cheekbones, gold or green oval eyes, upright rounded ears set high on the head, and a tapering tail with a blunt tip. The coat is short and sleek, with longer fur on the tail and lower belly
GROOMING: Little required
TEMPERAMENT: Active, sweet-natured, sociable
SIMILAR BREEDS: None

BRITISH SHORTHAIR

This is one of the oldest English breeds and it is a self-contained, self-reliant cat. Although easy-going in family life, it does not like being handled too much and is quite happy without a great deal of attention. It is reasonably quiet, with a soft voice, but does need regular grooming. The overall impression that this cat gives is of curves – it is solidly built, with a round head and rounded paws. Its coat is dense and plush and the classic and most popular colour is Blue, hence its original name. It now has a wide range of other colours, including White, Tortoiseshell, Black, all kinds of tabby and pointed colours. However, many of these new colours are not accepted by breed registries outside Great Britain.

ALTERNATIVE NAMES: British Blue
ORIGIN: United Kingdom
WEIGHT: 4–7.75 kg (9–17 lbs)
DESCRIPTION: Solidly built, compact, rounded cat with a broad chest, round head, medium ears with rounded tips, short strong legs with compact paws and a short, thick tail with a blunt tip. The coat is thick, dense and crisp and the large, round eyes are usually gold or copper.
GROOMING: Moderate grooming required
TEMPERAMENT: Easy-going, relaxed, reserved
SIMILAR BREEDS: American Shorthair is less stocky and compact; European Shorthair has a more triangular head with a well-defined muzzle. The earliest and classic colour of British Shorthair, British Blue, is sometimes confused with the Chartreux, which has slender legs and is less rounded

Above: British Shorthair Tortoiseshell and White
Below: British Shorthair Blue Spotted Tabby
Opposite: British Shorthair Silver Tabby

EUROPEAN SHORTHAIR

The European Shorthair was once classed as British Shorthair, but has been a separate breed since the early 1980s. The two breeds are very similar – as is the American Shorthair – but the European Shorthair can be distinguished by its rather lighter build and less rounded shape. It is not as popular or well known as the other two breeds, but it is a calm, self-contained, affectionate cat. It is quiet and undemanding and requires little grooming so is an ideal companion for those with heavy work commitments. The European Shorthair is available in a wide range of colours and patterns, including self and tortie colours, tabby and smokes. Most cats have eyes that match their coat, but some have unusual odd-coloured eyes.

ALTERNATIVE NAMES: Keltic Shorthair
ORIGIN: Europe
WEIGHT: 3–6.75 kg (7–15 lbs)
DESCRIPTION: Medium to large cat, with a rounded triangular head and well-defined muzzle, medium upright ears with rounded tips, muscular legs and a thick tail tapering to a rounded tip. The coat is short and dense, the hair standing up from the body
GROOMING: Little required
TEMPERAMENT: Intelligent, calm, quiet
SIMILAR BREEDS: British Shorthair is generally a more rounded, stocky cat; American Shorthair has a more rounded head with full cheeks

Above: European Brown Tabby cat
Opposite: Cream European Shorthair cat

CHARTREUX

Authorities believe that in the 1700s the Chartreux was the most common domestic cat across France, but by the 1800s it had almost become extinct. A colony was found on an island off Brittany but again in the late 1940s the breed almost died out; it was resurrected by crossing the remaining cats with British Blues and Blue Longhairs. The Chartreux is a very attractive cat, with a dense blue-grey coat and bright orange eyes; the coat and eye colour may take up to two years to develop fully. It has a gentle, affectionate disposition and likes to be around people – often following them around – and gets on very well with children and other animals. It is generally quiet, but does require regular grooming because of its thick coat.

ALTERNATIVE NAMES: None
ORIGIN: France
WEIGHT: 4–7.75 kg (9–17 lbs)
DESCRIPTION: Large, powerful cat, with a broad oval face, large round copper or gold eyes, medium ears set high on the head, short slender legs with small paws and a thick tail tapering to a rounded tip. The short to medium coat is luxuriously dense and is a distinctive bright blue-grey
GROOMING: Moderate grooming required
TEMPERAMENT: Tolerant, non-aggressive, calm
SIMILAR BREEDS: British Blue has sturdier legs and is generally more rounded, with fuller cheeks

SIAMESE

In North America most registries only class Siamese cats with the traditional point colours of Seal, Blue, Chocolate and Lilac as Siamese, other shorthair pointed colours are classed as Colourpoint Shorthair. All North American registries class cats without a pointed or colourpoint coat as Oriental Shorthair. In Britain and Australasia, the term Siamese covers all the shorthaired coat colours and patterns. The first Siamese came from Thailand (formerly Siam) in the 1870s, where both royalty and Buddhist monks held it in great esteem. It became fashionable to own one in the West and the breed was immensely popular until the mid 1950s. The Siamese is intelligent, active and very demanding – it likes a lot of playtime and lots of attention and strongly dislikes being left alone. It is good in a family situation, being affectionate and good with children.

ALTERNATIVE NAMES: Royal Cat; Royal Siamese; Colourpoint Shorthair
ORIGIN: Thailand
WEIGHT: 2.75–5 kg (6–11 lbs)
DESCRIPTION: Svelte, medium-size cat, with a long, triangular face, slanted, widely spaced blue eyes, large upright ears continuing the line of the face, long, slim but muscular legs and a long tail tapering to a fine tip. The pointed or colourpoint coat is very short, fine and glossy
GROOMING: Little required
TEMPERAMENT: Attention-seeking, energetic, intelligent
SIMILAR BREEDS: Oriental Shorthairs are Siamese without a pointed or colourpoint coat. Colourpoint Shorthairs are colourpoint Siamese in non-traditional colours

ORIENTAL SHORTHAIR

The Oriental Shorthair is the North American name for Siamese cats with no pointing. They may have solid colour coats in a wide range of colours, including the traditional Seal, Chocolate, Blue and Lilac, plus other colours such as Havana or Chestnut Brown, Cinnamon Apricot and Cream, or they can be Tortoiseshell, Tabby, Smoke, Shaded or Tipped in an equally wide range of colours. Oriental Shorthairs have green eyes, instead of the more usual blue. The solid White Oriental Shorthair is slightly different, in that it has its own name – Oriental White – and may have either green or blue eyes. In Britain, only White Orientals with blue eyes are accepted, and they are called Foreign White. Despite the different name, these cats are essentially Siamese and have all the same behaviour traits.

ALTERNATIVE NAMES: Egyptian Cat; Mau; Foreign Shorthair; Siamese, Foreign White
ORIGIN: United Kingdom
WEIGHT: 4–5.5 kg (9–12 lbs)
DESCRIPTION: Long-bodied, medium-size cat, with a long, triangular face, slanted, widely spaced green eyes, large upright ears continuing the line of the face, long, slim but muscular legs and a long tapering tail. The coat is very short, fine and glossy. White Oriental Shorthair may have blue eyes
GROOMING: Little required
TEMPERAMENT: Attention-seeking, inquisitive, gregarious
SIMILAR BREEDS: Siamese and Colourpoint Shorthair are Oriental Shorthair with pointed or colourpoint coats

COLOURPOINT SHORTHAIR

In Britain and Australasia, the term Siamese covers all the shorthaired coat colours and patterns. In North America, Colourpoint Shorthair is the name that some registries use for Siamese cats with pointing that is either in a non-traditional colour, or is patterned with tabby stripes or tortoiseshell. The Colourpoint Shorthair shares all the Siamese's characteristics, including the blue eyes. In some paler colours, such as Cream Point and Fawn Point, the pointing is very close to the body colour and so is very subtle, but the Cinnamon Point looks more like a traditional Siamese. In North America Tabby Points are also called Lynx Points.

ALTERNATIVE NAMES: Siamese; Royal Cat; Royal Siamese

ORIGIN: Thailand

WEIGHT: 2.75–5 kg (6–11 lbs)

DESCRIPTION: Svelte, medium-size cat with a long, triangular face, slanted, widely spaced blue eyes, large upright ears continuing the line of the face, long, slim but muscular legs and a long tail tapering to a fine tip. The pointed or colourpoint coat is very short, fine and glossy

GROOMING: Little required

TEMPERAMENT: Attention-seeking, energetic, intelligent

SIMILAR BREEDS: These cats are classed as Siamese outside North America

HAVANA BROWN

The Havana Brown has no connection with Cuba – except perhaps that it may have been named after the popular Cuban cigar. The first Havana Brown was bred in Britain, from a cross between a Persian-Siamese and a Siamese. This is another breed with a confusing name. The solid chocolate colour of the first kitten was designated Havana Brown, but the breed was registered in Britain as Chestnut Brown Foreign. In North America the breed was called Havana Brown, but imports from the UK breeding programme are now called Chestnut Oriental Shorthair. The cat itself is intelligent and affectionate, but quite demanding. It is not very vocal, and needs little grooming, but does like company and is a good lap cat.

ALTERNATIVE NAMES: Chestnut Brown Foreign; Chestnut Oriental Shorthair; Havana; Berkshire Brown; Reading Brown
ORIGIN: United Kingdom and United States
WEIGHT: 3–4.5 kg (7–10 lbs)
DESCRIPTION: Muscular, medium-size cat, with a distinctive rectangular muzzle, striking green oval eyes, large upright wide-set ears, medium-length legs with oval paws and a gently tapering tail. The coat is short, thick and an even mahogany brown in colour
GROOMING: Little required
TEMPERAMENT: Intelligent, sociable, playful
SIMILAR BREEDS: None

SNOWSHOE

The name Snowshoe comes from the distinct white markings on this breed's feet. It developed from crossing Siamese with bicoloured American Shorthairs, which gave this new breed a build that is a mix of the two. It is a medium-size, agile cat, with a rounded wedge-shape head and bright blue eyes. The coat comes in two patterns — mitted and bi-colour — and four colours, Seal, Chocolate, Blue and Lilac. The white feet may have come from either side — they once appeared in Siamese but were considered a fault and have been eradicated over many years of breeding. The Snowshoe is a playful and talkative cat, but it has a more pleasing voice than the Siamese. It is amiable and happy to be around children, but also content to be a pampered lap cat.

ALTERNATIVE NAMES: Silver Laces Cat
ORIGIN: United States
WEIGHT: 2.75–4.5 kg (6–10 lbs)
DESCRIPTION: Medium-size, agile cat, with a broadly wedge-shaped head, oval blue eyes, large ears continuing the line of the face, medium legs, and a slightly tapering tail. The short, smooth coat is subtly coloured, with white mittens or white markings on the toes, and a white inverted V on the face
GROOMING: Little required
TEMPERAMENT: Affectionate, amiable, friendly
SIMILAR BREEDS: None

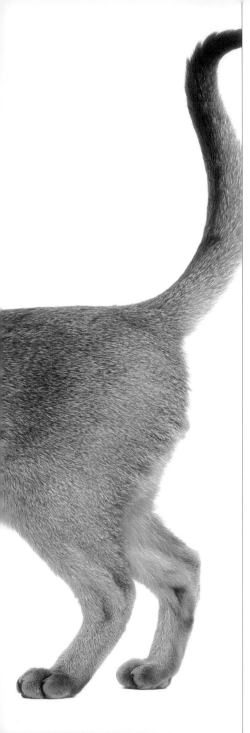

ABYSSINIAN

It is thought that the forebears of the Abyssinian were brought to Britain by troops returning after the Abyssinian War in the late 1800s, although this is not certain and some authorities have alternative theories. This breed's most striking feature is the beautiful ticked pattern on its tabby coat. The most common coat colour is a deep red-brown, known as Ruddy in the US and Usual in the UK, but pedigree animals also come in many other colours, including Red (Sorrel), Blue, Fawn and Silver. The Abyssinian is a sociable cat, happy around people and other animals, but is certainly not a lap cat because it likes its freedom and will not be happy if confined. It is generally quiet, but has a pleasant voice.

ALTERNATIVE NAMES: Algerian Cat; Ethiopian Cat

ORIGIN: Ethiopia

WEIGHT: 3.5–7.25 kg (8–16 lbs)

DESCRIPTION: Lithe, muscular cat, with a wedge-shaped head, large cupped and pointed ears, long slender legs and a gently tapering tail the same length as the body. The rounded almond-shaped eyes are gold or green. The coat is medium length and fine-textured

GROOMING: Little required

TEMPERAMENT: Attention-seeking, playful

SIMILAR BREEDS: Somali has a rounder head, longer hair and a fluffier tail

KORAT

A very attractive cat, with its silvery blue-grey coat and green to amber eyes, the Korat is also a symbol of good luck in its native Thailand. It is a muscular, compact cat with a heart-shaped face, but its innocent expression conceals a very strong-willed animal that likes to have things its own way. It is playful and likes company and lots of attention – although it tends to be shy with strangers – and hates being left on its own. It is not a vocal cat, and its shorthaired coat only needs minimal grooming. Despite its origins the Korat does not look anything like a Siamese in build and only comes in one solid colour. It is reasonably well known in North America, but otherwise rare outside Thailand.

ALTERNATIVE NAMES: SiSawat
ORIGIN: Thailand
WEIGHT: 3–4.5 kg (7–10 lbs)
DESCRIPTION: Medium size, heavily built, compact muscular cat, with a heart-shaped face, large, rounded yellow-green eyes, large ears rounded at the tips and sitting high on the head, and a tapering tail with a rounded tip. The short, glossy coat is blue-grey in colour, with silver tipping
GROOMING: Little required
TEMPERAMENT: Gentle, quiet, strong-willed
SIMILAR BREEDS: Russian Blue has a lighter build, a thicker, double coat and more emerald-green eyes

RUSSIAN BLUE – SHORTHAIR

The Russian Blue is traditionally a shorthaired cat, although longhaired versions do appear, which are sometimes classed as a separate breed, Nebelung. The thick, very soft, double coat of the Russian Blue cat is a rich blue-grey, with a silvery sheen, and is so dense that it stands away from the body. Some breeders have developed cats with pure black or white coats, which they have christened Black Russian and White Russian respectively, but they are controversial and not accepted by most registries. The Russian Blue is a gentle, shy cat, intelligent but sometimes rather flighty. It is very energetic but cautious, is not very vocal and can be quite self-contained and aloof.

ALTERNATIVE NAMES: American Blue; Archangel; Russian Shorthair; Foreign Blue
ORIGIN: Russia
WEIGHT: 2.75–5.5 kg (6–12 lbs)
DESCRIPTION: Lithe, graceful cat, with a rather triangular head, wide-spaced ears with pointed tips, almond-shaped, widely spaced green eyes, small, long muscular legs and a medium length tail tapering to a rounded tip. The blue-grey coat is short and dense and has silver-tipped hairs
GROOMING: Little required
TEMPERAMENT: Shy, affectionate, energetic
SIMILAR BREEDS: Nebelung has a longer coat and a fluffy tail

AMERICAN BURMESE

The American Burmese is a more rounded cat than the European Burmese. It is descended from a brown cat from Burma, which was bred to a Siamese. The rounded shape was a later development, and unfortunately sometimes results in cats being born with an inherited deformity of the skull that can be lethal. The coat is short and glossy, with the most common colour being Sable, although there are now a range of other self colours, including Champagne, Blue, Sable Tortie, Cinnamon and Platinum. The blue and silvery colours have a fawn undertone, which makes them warmer in tone than similar colours in other breeds. The American Burmese is relaxed in human company, but is not very vocal.

ALTERNATIVE NAMES: Burmese; Mandalay
ORIGIN: Myanmar (formerly Burma)
WEIGHT: 3.5–5.5 kg (8–12 lbs)
DESCRIPTION: Compact, muscular cat, with a rounded face, widely spaced, forward-tilting ears with rounded tips, medium-length slender legs and a medium-length tail. The rounded eyes are golden and the silky coat is short, fine and glossy
GROOMING: Little required
TEMPERAMENT: Affectionate, intelligent, playful
SIMILAR BREEDS: European Burmese has a more angular shape and wedge-shaped head

EUROPEAN BURMESE

Although the American Burmese and the European Burmese have common ancestors, they have developed in different ways on their different sides of the Atlantic. The European Burmese has a more angular, muscular shape and a more Oriental-looking head, with slanted eyes. It also has a wider range of colours, including an additional six: Red, Cream, Seal Tortie, Blue Tortie, Chocolate Tortie and Lilac Tortie. Some cats also have green eyes instead of the more usual yellow to amber. Despite these differences the two breeds have very similar temperaments, being loyal and friendly and enjoying human company. They are good with children and animals and make an ideal household pet.

ALTERNATIVE NAMES: Burmese; Foreign Burmese
ORIGIN: Myanmar (formerly Burma)
WEIGHT: 3–6.25 kg (7–14 lbs)
DESCRIPTION: Angular, well-muscled cat, with a wedge-shaped head, wide-set medium ears with rounded tips, slender legs with oval paws, a short, fine coat and a gently tapering tail with a rounded tip. The large, rounded yellow to amber eyes are widely spaced and slightly slanted
GROOMING: Little required
TEMPERAMENT: Intelligent, lively, friendly
SIMILAR BREEDS: American Burmese has a more rounded shape

ASIAN SHORTHAIR

The Asian Shorthair is a group, rather than a breed, and includes distinct breeds such as the Burmilla and the British Bombay. The group can be divided into Shaded (in which the hair is silvered for around half its length – these cats are known as Burmillas), Smokes (a coloured coat with a white undercoat – these cats were once called Burmoires), Selfs (a coat of only one colour – the British Bombay is a Black Self) and Tabby (a pattern of stripes, splotches and spots). The Asian Shaded were the first members of the Asian Shorthair group, after a Burmese mated with a Chinchilla Longhair. Each of the coat types in the Asian Shorthair group comes in a very wide range of colours.

ALTERNATIVE NAMES: Group includes Burmilla, British Bombay, Burmoires
ORIGIN: United Kingdom
WEIGHT: 4–7.25 kg (9–16 lbs)
DESCRIPTION: Medium-size, firmly muscled cat, with a short wedge-shaped face rounded at the top, large wide-spaced ears, medium-length legs with oval paws, and a medium to long tapering tail with a rounded end. The rounded, almond-shaped eyes can be any colour from gold to green
GROOMING: Moderate grooming required
TEMPERAMENT: Attention-seeking, even-tempered, relaxed
SIMILAR BREEDS: Burmilla is an Asian Shorthair with a light-coloured coat tipped with a contrasting colour; the British Bombay is an Asian Shorthair with a black coat. The American-bred Bombay is a separate breed, but also has a jet-black coat

BOMBAY (ASIAN SHORTHAIR)

The British Bombay is one of the original Asian Shorthair Self colours, although a range of other colours is now also found. It is a separate breed from the Bombay, although both include Burmese in their ancestry. Its ancestry includes non-pedigree cats, although it looks more like the Burmese in general shape. It has a pure black coat and eyes that may be any colour from green to gold. Like other Asian Shorthairs, the British Bombay is gregarious and active and not particularly vocal. Its sleek coat is dense and thick and needs regular grooming to keep it looking its best.

ALTERNATIVE NAMES: Asian Shorthair
ORIGIN: United Kingdom
WEIGHT: 4–7.25 kg (9–16 lbs)
DESCRIPTION: Medium-size, firmly muscled cat, with a short wedge-shaped face rounded at the top, large wide-spaced ears, medium-length legs with oval paws, and a medium to long tapering tail with a rounded end. The rounded, almond-shaped eyes can be any colour from gold to green and the coat is sleek and black
GROOMING: Moderate grooming required
TEMPERAMENT: Attention-seeking, even-tempered, relaxed
SIMILAR BREEDS: The American-bred Bombay is a separate breed that also has a jet-black coat, but has copper-gold eyes

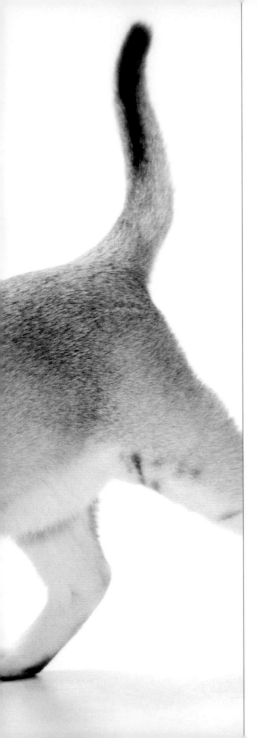

BURMILLA

The Burmilla is descended from a
Burmese and a Chinchilla Longhair
– its temperament and build are like
its Burmese side, while the unusual
shading of the coat comes from the
Chinchilla. Its short coat is light
underneath with the hairs tipped in
a contrasting colour to give the
attractive shaded effect; there is a
wide range of accepted colours,
including Chocolate, Red, Lilac,
Apricot, Blue Tortie and Caramel
Tortie. The Burmilla is also known
as Asian Shaded and is part of the
Asian Shorthair group. It is a
sociable, even-tempered,
affectionate cat, which likes to be
part of a family and enjoys the
company of children and other
animals. It likes a lot of attention,
but is not noisy or overly
demanding.

ALTERNATIVE NAMES: Asian Shaded
ORIGIN: United Kingdom
WEIGHT: 3.5–5.5 kg (8–12 lbs)
DESCRIPTION: Medium-size, muscular, compact
　　cat, with a wedge-shaped face and
　　rounded head, medium to large widely-
　　spaced and outward-pointing ears,
　　medium legs with oval paws and a long,
　　tapering tail with a rounded tip. The soft,
　　short coat is pale tipped with a darker
　　colour, and the rounded eyes range from
　　gold to green
GROOMING: Moderate grooming required
TEMPERAMENT: Affectionate, playful, sociable
SIMILAR BREEDS: Burmilla is part of the Asian
　　Shorthair group, which includes other coat
　　colours

BENGAL

Descended from a cross between a
wildcat – an Asian Leopard Cat –
and domestic cats, the Bengal has a
thick, luxurious coat. This is usually
spotted, rather like that of a
leopard, or marbled, with random
bands of colour, although a few cats
have a plain black coat. Both the
spotted and striped patterns are
asymmetrical, like that of a wild cat,
and not like the more symmetrical
markings of a domestic tabby.
Originally some cats also inherited
the wildcat's unpredictable
temperament, but breeding
programmes have concentrated on
developing a gentler nature. There
are relatively few Bengals around
the world, but it is popular with
breeders so numbers look set to
increase. The Bengal is a very lively
and active cat, but quite self-
contained and quiet.

ALTERNATIVE NAMES: Leopardettes
ORIGIN: United States
WEIGHT: 4.5–10 kg (10–22 lbs)
DESCRIPTION: Large, sleek, muscular cat, with
  a rounded but slightly elongated face,
  short rounded ears, wide-set oval eyes,
  medium-length muscular legs and a thick
  tail with a rounded tip that is carried low.
  The spotted or marbled coat is dense, thick
  and luxuriously soft
GROOMING: Little required
TEMPERAMENT: Active, intelligent, assertive
SIMILAR BREEDS: None

SNOW BENGAL

During the initial development of the Bengal, non-pedigree cats were used, crossed with the Asian Leopard Cat. These non-pedigree cats introduced Siamese pointing into the Bengal line, and although this normally would have been undesirable, it led to the beautiful coat colouring of the Snow Bengal and the attractive blue eyes. The Snow Bengal may have either a spotted or a marbled coat, but the background colour is White with an attractive snow-dusting over the coloured areas.

ALTERNATIVE NAMES: None
ORIGIN: United States
WEIGHT: 4.5–10 kg (10–22 lbs)
DESCRIPTION: Large, sleek, muscular cat, with a rounded but slightly elongated face, short rounded ears, wide-set oval, blue eyes, medium-length muscular legs and a thick tail with a rounded tip that is carried low. The coat is dense, thick and luxuriously soft
GROOMING: Little required
TEMPERAMENT: Active, intelligent, assertive
SIMILAR BREEDS: None

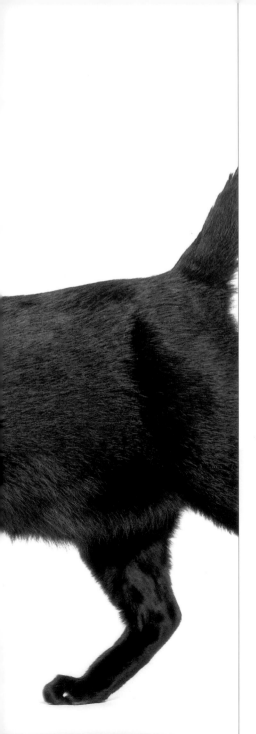

BOMBAY

This striking cat has a coat of pure jet black and bright copper-gold eyes – although sometimes Sable kittens appear because it is descended from crossing Black American Shorthairs with Sable Burmese. This is a cat that loves human company and warm places – its ideal position is on someone's lap. It is happy living in a family, comfortable with children and other animals, and its sleek coat is quite low-maintenance. It is also active and inquisitive and can be trained to walk on a leash like a dog, and to play fetch. The Bombay is quite rare outside North America, and may be confused with the British Bombay, which is an Asian Shorthair Self that is also pure black.

ALTERNATIVE NAMES: None
ORIGIN: United States
WEIGHT: 3–5 kg (7–11 lbs)
DESCRIPTION: Medium-size, heavy-boned, muscular cat, with a rounded face, wide ears rounded at the tip, medium-length sturdy legs and a medium-length thick tail. The jet-black coat is sleek, close-lying and shiny and the rounded eyes are copper to gold
GROOMING: Little required
TEMPERAMENT: Active, inquisitive, affectionate
SIMILAR BREEDS: Burmese are slightly smaller, with shorter body and legs. The British Bombay is an Asian Shorthair, and is a separate breed

EGYPTIAN MAU

Mau is the Egyptian word for 'cat' and the Egyptian Mau resembles cats shown in ancient Egyptian wall paintings. They are descended from cats brought from Cairo to Italy and then on to America – the entire North American breed was at first descended from only three cats, until others were brought from Egypt to extend the breeding pool. The Egyptian Mau has a distinctive coat, with very dark spots on a pale background. The spots range quite a lot in size, are not arranged in any discernible pattern and are clearly defined. This breed is well known in America but almost unknown in Europe. After selective breeding they have an even temperament and are energetic and sociable cats.

ALTERNATIVE NAMES: None
ORIGIN: Egypt and Italy
WEIGHT: 3–5 kg (7–11 lbs)
DESCRIPTION: Medium-size, well-muscled cat, with a rounded wedge-shaped face, round greenish eyes, medium to large upright ears, medium-length muscular legs and a medium-length gently tapering tail. The medium-length, fine silky coat is marked with clear randomly placed spots, which can be any shape or size
GROOMING: Little required
TEMPERAMENT: Intelligent, loyal, friendly
SIMILAR BREEDS: Oriental Shorthair with a spotted coat was once called Mau, but it is a different breed with rounded, evenly distributed spots

OCICAT

The first Ocicat was produced accidentally, when a Siamese was bred to a Siamese-Abyssinian cross in an attempt to produce a pointed Siamese with a ticked tabby pattern. The litter had the intended kittens, but also one spotted one that looked rather like an ocelot. A further mating produced more spotted kittens, and these were the basis of the new spotted breed. The Ocicat is a medium-size muscular cat, with darker spots on a pale background. Despite its rather wild appearance, it is a sociable cat with a dependable temperament, playful and good with children. It is very talkative and strongly dislikes being left alone, but can be trained to walk on the leash. This is still a comparatively rare breed in most areas.

ALTERNATIVE NAMES: Accicat; Ocelette
ORIGIN: United States
WEIGHT: 3.5–6.75 kg (8–15 lbs)
DESCRIPTION: Graceful, muscular, athletic cat, with a rounded wedge-shaped head, large erect ears set at an angle, slightly tilted almond-shaped eyes, medium-length muscular legs and a long slender tail. The short, sleek coat is spotted, rather like that of an ocelot
GROOMING: Little required
TEMPERAMENT: Sociable, playful, energetic
SIMILAR BREEDS: Egyptian Mau is also spotted, but the spots are darker, more random and well defined

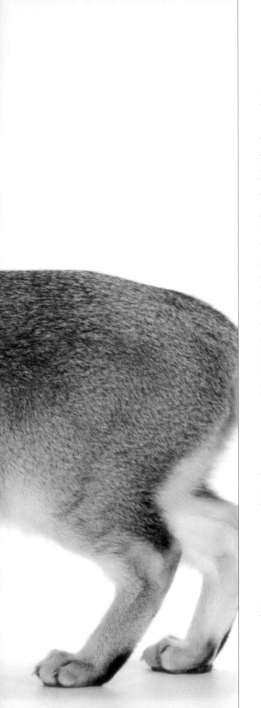

SINGAPURA

One of the smallest domestic cats, the Singapura has disputed origins. One story is that it was discovered on the streets of Singapore and that all registered cats are descended from street cats imported into North America. Others hold that breeders created the Singapura by crossing an Abyssinian with a Burmese. Whatever its true origins, the Singapura is a very attractive cat. Its short, sleek coat only comes in one colour – Sepia Agouti, with brown tabby ticking on an ivory background across most of its body, a pale stomach, chest and muzzle and tabby markings on the face and legs. It is a quiet, affectionate cat but full of energy, and it craves human companionship so does not like being left alone.

ALTERNATIVE NAMES: Singapore River Cat; Singapore Drain Cat
ORIGIN: Singapore/United States
WEIGHT: 2.25–4 kg (5–9 lbs)
DESCRIPTION: Small, stocky cat, with a rounded head, large cupped ears angled outwards, strong legs and a slender tail almost the same length as the body. The almond-shaped eyes are hazel, yellow or green, with a black outline, and the short coat is pale ivory with darker ticking
GROOMING: Little required
TEMPERAMENT: Quiet, affectionate, intelligent
SIMILAR BREEDS: None

TONKINESE

The Tonkinese is the result of a Siamese-Burmese cross and is a good blend of the two breeds. It is a medium-size cat, with a muscular body and a rounded head. The favoured pattern for show cats is mink with aquamarine eyes, but cats also come in self and pointed patterns, which are used in breeding programmes. There is a range of colours, including Brown, Chocolate, Blue, Lilac and Cream. The Tonkinese is an entertaining cat, sociable, intelligent and curious. They are full of energy and talkative, but equally happy as family companions or as lap cats. They do need plenty of attention and dislike being left alone, so they fit better into a busy household. Although they are not yet widely known, they are quickly gaining in popularity.

ALTERNATIVE NAMES: Chocolate Siamese; Golden Siamese
ORIGIN: North America
WEIGHT: 2.75–4.5 kg (6–10 lbs)
DESCRIPTION: Heavy, muscular cat, with a rounded wedge-shaped head, blue-green eyes, tall ears with rounded tips, slim muscular legs and a tail the same length as the body. The short, silky coat lies close to the body
GROOMING: Little required
TEMPERAMENT: Sociable, affectionate, intelligent
SIMILAR BREEDS: None

BREEDS:
CATS WITH SPECIAL
CHARACTERISTICS

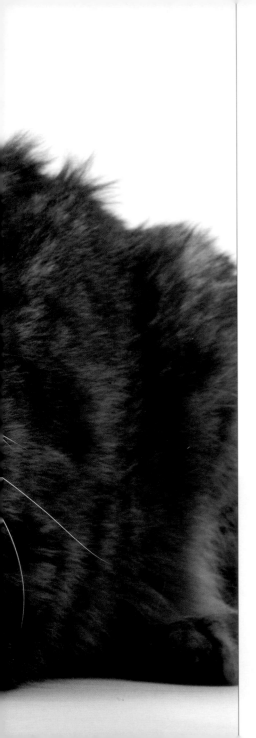

AMERICAN CURL

The most remarkable feature of the American Curl is its ears, the tips of which turn back. The breed is descended from a stray cat in which the curled ears were a spontaneous mutation, which proved to be caused by a dominant gene. Kittens are born with normal ears, but by the time they are three weeks old the curled ears will have developed if they are destined to have them. The coat comes in all colours and patterns, and may be long or short, although the shorthaired is less common. The American Curl is friendly and loves to be around humans, being happy as a lap cat and enjoying the company of children.

ALTERNATIVE NAMES: None

ORIGIN: United States

WEIGHT: 3–5.5 kg (7–12 lbs)

DESCRIPTION: Medium-size, muscular cat, with a rounded wedge-shaped face, large walnut-shaped eyes, distinctive backward-curling ears, medium-length legs and a tapering tail the same length as the body. The Curl can be either shorthaired or longhaired; the longhaired variety has a plume-like tail

GROOMING: Little required

TEMPERAMENT: Friendly, affectionate, even-tempered

SIMILAR BREEDS: None

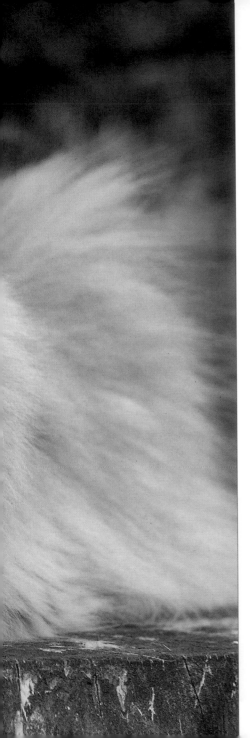

HIGHLAND FOLD

This breed is the longhaired version of the Scottish Fold, but is considerably less common. Although longhaired kittens appear regularly, the folded-ear ones cannot be bred to each other as this leads to inherited joint problems, and outcross breeds are not available. The coat of the Highland Fold is medium to long, with the hair longest on the ruff, down the rear legs and the tail. The coat comes in a wide variety of colours and patterns and needs grooming regularly to remove loose hair and keep it looking its best. The distinctive folded ears bend forward to lie flat against the head, and are caused by a dominant mutant gene. Kittens are born with normal ears, but the fold develops over the first three months. The Highland Fold has a gentle temperament and is good with children.

ALTERNATIVE NAMES: Coupari; Longhaired Scottish Fold
ORIGIN: Scotland
WEIGHT: 4.5–6 kg (10–13 lbs)
DESCRIPTION: Medium-size, round cat, with a rounded head, short neck, large, round widely spaced eyes, sturdy legs and a large fluffy tail. The soft coat is medium to long and stands away from the body, and the distinctive ears fold forward flat against the head
GROOMING: Moderate grooming required
TEMPERAMENT: Quiet, sweet- natured, sociable
SIMILAR BREEDS: Scottish Fold is identical but shorthaired

SCOTTISH FOLD

The distinctive folded ears of this breed bend forward to lie flat against the head, and are caused by a dominant mutant gene. Kittens are usually born with some degree of fold, but it develops over the first three months – it can vary from ears that merely bend forward to those that lie fully flat. Folds cannot be bred to Folds, due to the danger of crippling inherited bone problems, but the gene that causes the folded ears is dominant, so Folds can be cross-bred to straight-eared cats. The coat of the Scottish Fold is short and dense, with the hair standing away from the body, and it has a long, rather fluffy tail. The coat comes in a wide variety of colours and patterns and should be brushed once a week to remove loose hair. The Scottish Fold has a sweet-natured, gentle temperament and is good with children, but it can be quiet and self-contained.

ALTERNATIVE NAMES: Scottish Lop
ORIGIN: Scotland
WEIGHT: 2.75–5.5 kg (6–12 lbs)
DESCRIPTION: Medium-size, round cat, with a rounded head, short neck, large, round, widely spaced eyes, sturdy legs and a large fluffy tail. The soft coat is medium to long and stands away from the body, and the distinctive ears fold forward flat against the head
GROOMING: Little required
TEMPERAMENT: Placid, sweet tempered, sociable
SIMILAR BREEDS: Highland Fold is identical, but longhaired

AMERICAN WIREHAIR

Descended from a single male farm cat that was born with a dense wiry coat, the American Wirehair is very similar to the American Shorthair in disposition. Since the two breeds were often crossed, they also have a similar range of colours and patterns, but the Wirehair's unusual coat sets it apart – it is dense and coarse, with springy, crimped hair. The most prized cats also have curly whiskers. Kittens may not have a very curly coat at birth, but this can continue to develop during the first year. The American Wirehair is an easy-going cat that is good with children and enjoys being handled. It is found throughout the United States and Canada, but is quite rare in other areas of the world.

ALTERNATIVE NAMES: None
ORIGIN: United States
WEIGHT: 3.5–6.25 kg (8–14 lbs)
DESCRIPTION: Medium to large, well-muscled cat, with rounded head, medium-size ears rounded at the tip, large wide-spaced eyes, sturdy legs with compact paws and a tapering tail with a rounded tip. The distinctive coat is coarse, springy and dense, with thin, crimped hairs
GROOMING: Little required
TEMPERAMENT: Easy-going, busy, friendly
SIMILAR BREEDS: None

CORNISH REX

The unusual wavy coat of the
Cornish Rex first occurred as a
natural mutation, but breeders then
worked to strengthen the gene and
increase coat colours. Inbreeding
often causes health problems, so
other breeds were also introduced to
try and avoid these. However the
soft, wavy coat is very delicate and
does not protect the cat from cold or
sun. The Cornish Rex is very playful
and affectionate, full of energy and
talkative. The North American
standard for this breed calls for a
leaner cat, with the spine arched and
the belly held high, and larger ears,
while the British standard requires a
flatter head, smaller ears and a
straight nose. The coat curls in rows
of waves, giving a 'washboard' effect,
and comes in a wide range of colours
and patterns, including pointed,
tortoiseshell and smoke.

ALTERNATIVE NAMES: Coodle; English Rex
ORIGIN: United Kingdom
WEIGHT: 2.75–4 kg (6–9 lbs)
DESCRIPTION: Slender cat, with a large oval
   head, slanted oval eyes, large, dramatic
   cupped ears set high on the head, a broad
   chest, long, slender legs and a long, slender
   tail with a pointed tip. The distinctive short,
   wavy coat is velvet-soft and easily damaged
GROOMING: Little required
TEMPERAMENT: Playful, affectionate, acrobatic
SIMILAR BREEDS: Devon Rex has a more
   wedge-shaped head, is less elongated and
   its coat is more rippled than wavy

DEVON REX

Although at first sight there are some similarities between the Devon Rex and the Cornish Rex, their distinctive coats are caused by a different mutation so they cannot be crossbred. The Devon Rex is a stockier cat than the Cornish Rex, and its coat has a softer curl, more like a ripple than distinct waves. The Devon Rex's coat was also the result of a spontaneous mutation, but inbreeding was needed to establish the rippled coat because the gene that causes it is recessive – although other breeds were then introduced for health reasons and to add other colours. The coat is now found in a wide variety of colours and patterns, including pointed, tortoiseshell and tabby. The Devon Rex is one of life's clowns – active, acrobatic, playful and affectionate. They need to be indoor cats, as their delicate coats do not protect them from cold and sun.

ALTERNATIVE NAMES: Butterfly Rex
ORIGIN: United Kingdom
WEIGHT: 2.75–4 kg (6–9 lbs)
DESCRIPTION: Slender but muscular cat, with a wedge-shaped head, full cheeks and a defined chin, large eyes, large low-set ears with pointed tips, a broad chest, long slender legs, and a long, tapering tail. The distinctive short, soft, curled and rippled coat is easily damaged
GROOMING: Little required
TEMPERAMENT: Playful, affectionate, full of fun
SIMILAR BREEDS: Cornish Rex has an oval head, is more elongated and its coat is more wavy than rippled

LAPERM – LONGHAIR

The LaPerm is an unusual-looking cat, with its long hair in ringlets all over its body. The first cat was a spontaneous mutation, a single bald kitten in a litter of farmyard cats that later grew a coat of long, soft, curly hair. The gene that caused the curls proved to be dominant, so outcrossing can be used to keep the gene pool varied and healthy. The coat comes in a wide range of colours and patterns, and needs regular grooming to keep it in good condition. LaPerm and Selkirk Rex are the only two longhaired curly cats recognized by breed registries. There is also a shorthaired version of LaPerm, which has a soft wavy coat as the hair does not grow long enough to form ringlets. This is an outgoing, affectionate and inquisitive cat, which is happy as a lap cat but is also true to its farmyard origins, being an excellent hunter.

ALTERNATIVE NAMES: Alpaca Cat; Dalles LaPerm
ORIGIN: United States
WEIGHT: 3–5 kg (7–11 lbs)
DESCRIPTION: Medium size, heavy cat, with a broad head with prominent rounded muzzle, wide, almond-shaped, slanted eyes, medium ears with rounded tips, muscular legs and a long, tapering, plumed tail. The unusual coat is curled in ringlets, with long, thick, silky hair, and the whiskers may also curl
GROOMING: Moderate grooming required
TEMPERAMENT: Affectionate, inquisitive, active
SIMILAR BREEDS: Selkirk Rex Longhaired also has a long, curly coat, but is much more rounded in general shape, with smaller, wider-set ears

Above and opposite: The LaPerm's coat comes in a variety of colours and patterns but the kitten may go through a bald stage before the coat develops.

SELKIRK REX – LONGHAIR

The curly-haired kitten that founded the Selkirk Rex breed not only carried the dominant gene for a curly coat, but recessive genes for longhair and pointing. There are therefore both shorthaired and longhaired versions, and the two are not formally separated by breed registries. The coat of the longhaired Selkirk Rex is soft and plush, growing in loose ringlets, and it comes in a variety of colours and patterns. As in the shorthaired variety, kittens are born with curly hair and whiskers, but lose these for a sparse, straight coat until the curls come back in adulthood. The longhaired Selkirk Rex can be crossed with other longhaired cats, so the gene pool is refreshed and kept healthy. The coat is at its best in cats descended from one rexed and one longhaired parent.

ALTERNATIVE NAMES: None

ORIGIN: United States

WEIGHT: 3.5–5 kg (8–11 lbs)

DESCRIPTION: Medium-build, muscular cat, with a round head and short muzzle, widely spaced, pointed ears, large round eyes, medium legs and a thick tail with a rounded tip. The thick, soft coat is medium-length and grows in loose curls

GROOMING: Moderate grooming required

TEMPERAMENT: Tolerant, sociable

SIMILAR BREEDS: LaPerm longhaired is the only other longhaired rexed breed, but is a more elongated and less rounded cat

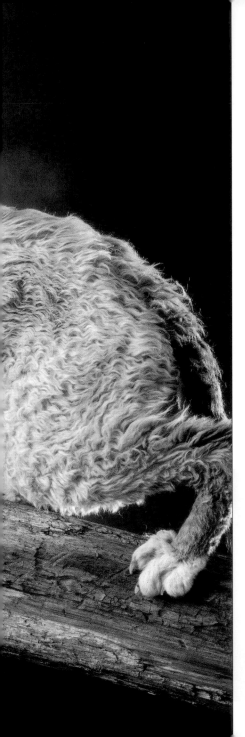

SELKIRK REX – SHORTHAIR

The founder of this breed was a curly-haired kitten, the only one in the litter, the result of a spontaneous mutation that proved to be caused by a dominant gene. This means that the breed can be outcrossed with other breeds to keep the gene pool varied and healthy. The new breed was named after the Selkirk Mountains in Wyoming, since the kitten was born nearby. The coat of the Selkirk Rex is soft and plush and grows in loose curls and it comes in a variety of colours and patterns. Kittens are born with curly hair and whiskers, but lose these for a sparse, straight coat until the curls come back in adulthood. The Selkirk Rex is a tolerant and easy-going animal, self-contained but good with children. Its coat needs minimal grooming and it is not very vocal.

ALTERNATIVE NAMES: None
ORIGIN: United States
WEIGHT: 3.5–5 kg (8–11 lbs)
DESCRIPTION: Medium-build, muscular cat, with a round head and short muzzle, widely spaced, pointed ears, large round eyes, medium legs and a thick tail with a rounded tip. The thick, soft coat is soft and plush and grows in loose curls
GROOMING: Moderate grooming required
TEMPERAMENT: Tolerant, sociable
SIMILAR BREEDS: LaPerm shorthaired is a more elongated and less rounded cat. Cornish Rex and Devon Rex are both more Oriental in appearance

CYMRIC

Despite its name, which comes from the Welsh word for Wales, the Cymric was bred in North America. Manx cats sometimes produced longhaired kittens, and breeders worked to establish a separate longhair breed. Like the Manx, the Cymric may have no tail (known as 'rumpies') a vestigial tail (known as 'stumpies') or a short tail (known as 'longies'). It is also prone to the same inherited health problems as the Manx – the gene for the lack of a tail also causes spinal defects. The Cymric is not recognized as a separate breed in Britain. Like the Manx, it is a friendly, relaxed cat, happy with human company and good with children. It is not particularly vocal, but does need regular grooming to keep its coat in good condition.

ALTERNATIVE NAMES: Longhaired Manx
ORIGIN: North America
WEIGHT: 4–5.5 kg (9–12 lbs)
DESCRIPTION: Medium-size, sturdy, well-muscled cat, with a rounded head, round eyes set at an angle, medium ears with rounded tips, sturdy legs with the forelegs shorter than the hindlegs, and no tail. The coat is dense, soft and medium-length, becoming longer towards the rump
GROOMING: Moderate grooming required
TEMPERAMENT: Affectionate, even-tempered
SIMILAR BREEDS: Manx is the same breed, but has short hair

MANX

The Manx is well known throughout the world as the cat with no tail. In fact it may have no tail (a 'rumpy') a vestigial tail (a 'stumpy') or a short tail (a 'longy'). The gene for the lack of a tail also causes spinal defects, so the Manx is prone to inherited health problems and some cats have a distinctive 'bunny-hop' walk. This is considered a defect by North American registries. The first Manx was a spontaneous mutation, but since it occurred on an island with a limited breeding pool, the trait became established. The Manx is a friendly, relaxed cat, happy with human company and good with children. It is not particularly vocal, but does need regular grooming to keep its coat in good condition. Manx cats sometimes produce longhaired kittens, and breeders have established a separate longhair breed, the Cymric.

ALTERNATIVE NAMES: None
ORIGIN: Isle of Man
WEIGHT: 4–5 kg (9–11 lbs)
DESCRIPTION: Medium-size, solidly built cat, with a large, round head, tall ears with rounded tips, round eyes set at a slight angle, short powerful legs and no tail. The hindlegs are longer than the forelegs, so the back arches up towards the rump. The double coat is short, thick and glossy
GROOMING: Little required
TEMPERAMENT: Relaxed, friendly
SIMILAR BREEDS: Cymric is the longhaired version of the Manx

JAPANESE BOBTAIL – SHORTHAIR

The shorthair version of the Japanese Bobtail is the more common of the two versions. Its tail has a fan of thick hair, and looks more like that of a rabbit than a pom-pom. The breed is very common in its homeland, Japan, where it is a symbol for good luck. It is now also well known in North America, although still quite rare in Britain. The bobbed tail is caused by a recessive gene, but as Japan provided a restricted area for breeding the gene had a chance to flourish. The most prized coat colour is tortoiseshell and white, known as Mi-ke in Japan and Calico in America. These cats usually have blue or gold eyes, but sometimes odd-eyed cats appear that are even more valued. Like the longhair, the shorthair is an intelligent, happy and gregarious cat.

ALTERNATIVE NAMES: None
ORIGIN: Japan
WEIGHT: 2.75–4 kg (6–9 lbs)
DESCRIPTION: Slender, muscular cat, with a long body, broad triangular head, large upright ears set wide apart, large oval eyes and high cheekbones, long slender legs and a medium-short, silky coat. The short tail has a fan of hair, making a fluffy pom-pom
GROOMING: Little required
TEMPERAMENT: Gregarious, intelligent, mischievous
SIMILAR BREEDS: Japanese Bobtail Longhair is identical but has longer hair

KURILE ISLAND BOBTAIL

The Kurile Island Bobtail is a breed that has developed naturally on the isolated Kurile Island chain, which is between Japan and Russia. It was only discovered recently, but has probably been in existence since the early 18th century. It has a small stumpy tail, the result of a natural mutation that so far does not seem to have any unpleasant side effects on the cat's health. The tail is short and curled and is always carried high – it is covered with a full tuft of thick fur and looks rather like a fluffy pom-pom. The breed is registered only in Russia, but is known in North America, although still rare in Britain. This is a busy and gregarious cat, not very vocal but fond of human company, although it likes to retain its independence.

ALTERNATIVE NAMES: None
ORIGIN: Kurile Islands
WEIGHT: 3–5 kg (7–11 lbs)
DESCRIPTION: Medium-size, sturdy well-muscled cat, with a broad head, medium upright ears, oval eyes slightly tilted, a distinct break in profile at the nose, sturdy but quite slender legs and a semi-long, silky coat. The short tail is covered in thick hair, and is curled and carried high
GROOMING: Moderate grooming required
TEMPERAMENT: Gregarious, friendly
SIMILAR BREEDS: Japanese Bobtail longhair is similar but often carries its tail low and is less sturdy with shorter and thinner hair

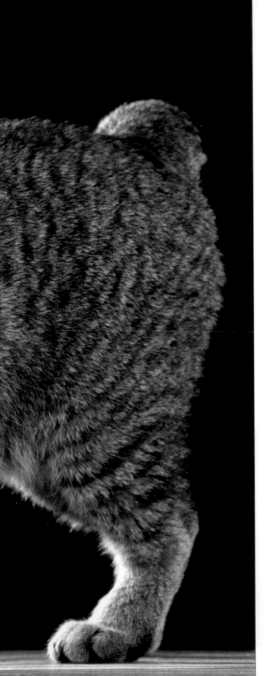

PIXIE-BOB

With its wild looks, the Pixie-Bob resembles the North American Bobcat, and is supposed to be descended from the mating of wild bobcats and domestic barn cats in rural areas, although this theory has never been proved. The Pixie-Bob is a solid, muscular cat, with short thick fur marked in either a spotted or rosette tabby pattern. The most common colour is Brown, although some other colours do appear. Although this cat does seem to have a dependable temperament it does not like to share its home with other animals and it strongly dislikes any change to its routine. The breed is only recognized by one North American registry, the TICA.

ALTERNATIVE NAMES: None
ORIGIN: North America
WEIGHT: 4–7.75 kg (9–17 lbs)
DESCRIPTION: Medium to large, solid cat, with a wide rounded head, deep-set eyes, rounded ears set back, sturdy legs and a short tapering tail carried low. The coat is short and thick, with tabby markings
GROOMING: Little required
TEMPERAMENT: Quiet, playful, self-contained
SIMILAR BREEDS: None

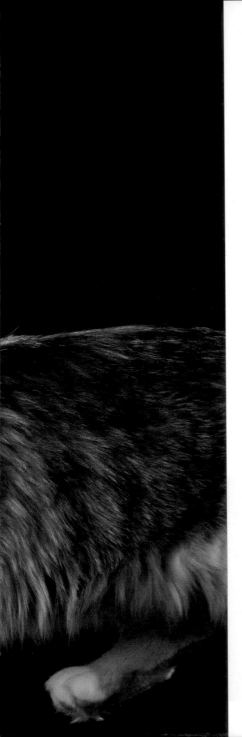

MUNCHKIN – LONGHAIR

Although controversial among both registries and some breeders, the Munchkin is becoming established as a popular new breed. Its defining characteristic is its short legs, which only raise the body a short way off the ground. In most species dwarfs are prone to arthritis or back and hip problems, but Munchkin breeders claim that the cats suffer no side effects. The breed was subjected to rigorous health tests by registries before it was accepted, but some breeders still consider them to look strange and not like a cat. The first Munchkin was a spontaneous mutation, and it was bred to non-pedigree cats to establish the trait. These are confident, friendly and talkative cats, easy-going and great with children. They come in all colours and patterns, and in both long- and shorthair.

ALTERNATIVE NAMES: Kangaroo Cat; Louisiana Creole Cat
ORIGIN: United States
WEIGHT: 2.75–4 kg (6–9 lbs)
DESCRIPTION: Medium-size muscular cat, with a triangular head, medium, upright ears, large, walnut-shape eyes, a thick, long coat and a gently tapering tail with a rounded tip. The distinctive short legs are well muscled and not misshapen; the paws turn outwards slightly
GROOMING: Moderate grooming required
TEMPERAMENT: Confident, intelligent, inquisitive
SIMILAR BREEDS: Munchkin Shorthair is the same breed but with short hair

MUNCHKIN – SHORTHAIR

The shorthaired version of the Munchkin is identical to the longhair except for the length of the coat. In a breed that has been established by outcrossing with non-pedigree cats it was inevitable that a wide range of coat types, colours and patterns would appear. The Munchkin's defining characteristic is its short legs, and the shorthaired version looks rather like a feline version of the Dachshund. Some breeders are now working to achieve a rexed coat or a cat with curled ears. Despite its short legs, the Munchkin can run, groom itself and climb trees, but finds it difficult to jump up to any height. They are confident, friendly and talkative cats, easy-going and great with children.

ALTERNATIVE NAMES: Kangaroo Cat; Louisiana Creole Cat
ORIGIN: United States
WEIGHT: 2.75–4.5 kg (6–10 lbs)
DESCRIPTION: Medium-size muscular cat, with a triangular head, medium, upright ears, large, walnut-shape eyes, a short, thick coat and a gently tapering tail with a rounded tip. The distinctive short legs are well-muscled and not misshapen, with outward-turned paws
GROOMING: Little required
TEMPERAMENT: Confident, intelligent, inquisitive
SIMILAR BREEDS: Munchkin Longhair is the same breed but with long hair

SPHYNX

The Sphynx is possibly the most well known of the hairless breeds, being recognized in both America and in Great Britain. It is descended from several occurrences of a natural mutation — hairless cats born to a farm cat and to a stray, which were then bred to a Devon Rex. The gene for hairlessness proved stronger than that for rexed hair, and the Sphynx became established as a breed. Despite its initially rather odd looks, with wrinkled skin and large, bat-like ears, the Sphynx is an easy-going cat with an appealing disposition that soon wins admirers. It is not truly hairless — its chamois-leather-like skin has a soft peach fuzz — and it needs rubbing with a chamois leather or shampooing regularly to remove the natural oils that can otherwise build up on the skin. The Sphynx is susceptible to sun and to cold so it should be kept as an indoor cat, but it is a good companion to children and other animals.

ALTERNATIVE NAMES: Canadian Hairless; Moonstone Cat
ORIGIN: NORTH America/Europe
WEIGHT: 3.5–5.5 kg (8–12 lbs)
DESCRIPTION: Rounded, muscular cat, with a round wedge-shaped head, large round eyes, oversize ears, long muscular legs and a slender tapering tail. The coat appears hairless, but often has a fine downy covering
GROOMING: Moderate grooming required
TEMPERAMENT: Affectionate, easy-going, playful
SIMILAR BREEDS: Peterbald is very similar in appearance

CHOOSING AND CARING FOR YOUR CAT

CHOOSING A CAT

O nce you have made the decision to own a cat, you need to choose which cat to have. It does not necessarily have to be a pedigree breed – ordinary cats make excellent pets. You will also need to know how to care for it on a day to day basis, and what to do in case of accident or emergency.

An important thing to consider right at the start is how much time you will be spending at home. Some cats are happier than others to be left alone for long periods. If you are going to be away from home for more than four hours a day on a regular basis, it would certainly be better not to have a very young kitten, which may be bored and unhappy on its own and certainly get into mischief. If you do have to leave a kitten alone for short periods on a regular basis, consider getting two as they will keep each other company. If you do, choose littermates if possible, as they will be used to being with each other.

Everyone in the family needs to be consulted in the decision to have a cat – they will all be involved to some extent with feeding, cleaning the litter tray and maybe grooming. Some people are allergic to cats, or rather to the protein in a cat's saliva. As part of its grooming routine a cat covers its coat with saliva so to minimize the effect you can wipe the coat daily with a clean damp sponge – although this will not completely overcome the problem. If you have children they need to understand just what will be required and how to treat a cat. Very young children must be supervised at all times at first, both for their own and for the animal's safety. Other pets may also need to be considered – most dogs will accept a cat into their home, but introductions should be carefully made and both animals need to get used to each other. If you have birds, hamsters or goldfish you will need to make sure they don't become a tasty snack. Remember a cat can live for 15 to

Above:Young children should be supervised with a new kitten.

20 years – which is a long time to be sharing your home with a bad decision, so take some time to make the right choice.

There are several sources you can try to find a cat. Taking in a stray, responding to an advert or buying from a pet shop are full of uncertainties, as you will not know anything about the cat's history so will be unable to judge if its temperament will fit in with your family. Rescue centres take in stray and unwanted cats and try to find them a good home – they are a better source for a family pet as they will have checked out the animal's health, had it neutered and given it all the necessary vaccinations. Obtaining a pet from this source also means that you will be giving a home to an animal that might otherwise be put down. These centres only occasionally have kittens – most of their animals are older cats, but they still make ideal pets. Make sure that any cat you are offered is used to living with humans – adult feral cats may accept a home with regular food, but will

Above: A family meet their new pet at a cat sanctuary.
Opposite: There are various designs of food bowl on the market.

not be comfortable with too much human contact. The best source for your pet is perhaps a reputable breeder, who will have a full health history for any cat you buy and will be able to predict its temperament with some accuracy. If you choose a pedigree animal, make sure it has no hereditary illnesses and is free of any viruses. Top show animals are unlikely to be offered for sale or will be very expensive, but the breeder will have many other cats that are not suitable for showing or breeding for some reason but which will be perfectly good pets.

When choosing a cat, look carefully for any signs of ill health. It should not be too thin or too fat, the coat should be healthy looking and the eyes and ears free from any discharge. If choosing a kitten, it may have a slight potbelly but a distended belly can be a sign of disease. Pick one that is inquisitive and moves towards you – those that hang back or appear particularly quiet may be ill or disturbed in some way.

If you don't have a full health history for your new cat for any reason, have it checked out by a vet as soon as possible, and arrange for all the necessary vaccinations if they have not already been done. Don't forget to have the animal neutered at the same time – there are already too many abandoned and unwanted cats in the world. Also make sure your cat has identification – either a simple tag or capsule on the collar with your name and address, or a microchip inserted under the skin.

Equipment

You will not need much basic equipment to look after your cat. Each cat in your home should have its own food dish, but the water dish can be shared. Both dishes should sit low enough for the cat to eat and drink comfortably, but have high enough sides to keep the food or water inside. Metal, glass or china are best – make sure you choose something fairly substantial that will not tip over easily. Plastic dishes may not be heavy enough to stay put and are difficult to clean properly.

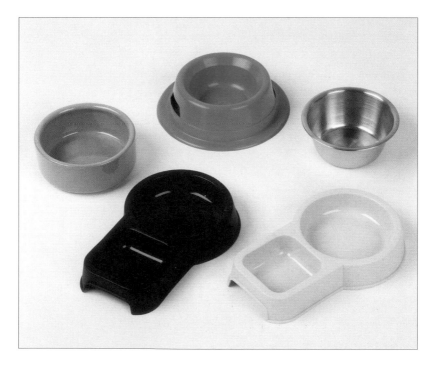

Automatic feeders that release a measured amount of food each day are useful if you need to be away for several days at a time – particularly if your cat is a greedy type and will eat several days' worth of food all at once. If the cat has access to more than one floor in your house, place a water bowl on each floor, although it is not necessary to have one for each cat.

There are several types of litter tray on the market, including a simple tray, a tray with a cover and even ones with a built-in machine to sift the waste and put it into a bag for disposal. The simple ones are usually the best and the least expensive, but other types do have their plus points. The hooded variety is intended to cut down on smells, but if it is not cleaned often enough the smell inside can stop a cat from using it. However, it does offer some privacy and quiet to a cat in a busy household, and some cats may prefer this. The self-cleaning type is very convenient for busy people, but the mechanism may frighten the cat. Find a type of cat litter your cat likes and try to stick to it – cats have a very sensitive sense of smell, and may stop using the tray if it smells unfamiliar.

Your cat will need somewhere to sleep, but will probably choose its own spot. You can buy a special animal bed, but the cat may not use it so it may be better to wait and see if it is needed. If you do buy one, make sure it is washable. A cat carrier is a good investment – even if you will not be travelling any distance with your cat, you will need it for trips to the vet. If it is on hand most of the time you can leave it out with some soft bedding and maybe a favourite toy inside, so the cat regards it as a safe place rather than a scary one. Carriers come in various types, but you just need to be sure it is easy to clean and has nothing on the inside that the cat could harm itself on.

For grooming a shorthaired cat you will need a comb with wide teeth, a flea comb and a bristle or rubber toothed brush. For a longhaired cat you will need the comb and flea comb, a brush with stiff bristles or a pin brush, and blunt scissors for removing matting.

A scratching post will be useful to prevent your cat scratching the furniture.

Opposite: Grooming tools (from top): bristle and pin brush, slicker brush and two different flea combs.

UNDERSTANDING
YOUR CAT

ost of the things that you see cats do can be explained by looking at their behaviour in the wild, although a few traits may just be the quirks of an individual animal. Like humans, cats have their own personality and like to do slightly different things. However, all cats need to hunt, they want to mate and if they have kittens they will care for and feed them.

Behaviour

To be successful at hunting, a cat needs to have learned the skills from another cat, most usually its mother while it was still a kitten. If it has not learned to hunt properly when it is very young then it will never be an efficient predator – but this will not mean that it loses the instinct to hunt, which is inborn. Kittens playing with toys are actually play-hunting – stalking, biting or pawing at inanimate toys, or chasing after anything that moves. Sometimes a cat will catch a small bird or rodent but then appear to play with it cruelly, batting it around with its paws, or letting the victim escape and then re-catching it. This is not deliberate cruelty, however – the movement of the prey is stimulating the cat's predatory instincts, but it has simply not learned what to do next – it cannot kill quickly and efficiently as it has not been taught how to.

When cats scratch furniture it is not just a way to sharpen their claws. In the wild, the scratch marks are always in a highly visible place as they are a non-threatening indication that a territory is occupied. Providing a scratching post as an alternative for your cat to use will therefore only work if it is kept in a prominent position – hiding it away in a corner is no good, as to the cat there is no point in scratching something that cannot be seen and understood.

The mating instinct can bring its own problems apart from unwanted kittens. If male cats are not neutered they will spray urine to mark their territory, even inside the home, and the smell can be extremely hard to eradicate. Even cats that normally live indoors will try to get outside to roam around looking for a

Above: Kittens enjoy playing with more or less anything, but an older cat will prefer interactive toys.

mate. Outside they will get into fights with other male cats defending territory, which can lead to quite serious injuries and infections. Neutering does stop most of this behaviour, but only if it done before the cat is around eight months old. Female cats only present problems when they are in heat – they may also spray, will become very noisy and will rub against objects continuously. Again neutering needs to be carried out before the female is eight months old, or you may find a litter of kittens is on the way. A less unpleasant kind of marking is often taken as a sign of affection by a cat's owner – which it is, but the cat is also marking you as its own. When a cat rubs its head against your face – known as head bunting – licks your face or hands, or wraps its body around your legs, curling its tail as if in caress, it is marking you with scent-producing glands on the face, neck, rump and at the base of the tail.

Above: A cat can be trained not to jump on surfaces where it is not welcome, but it is important to provide alternatives.

Although establishing its territory is important to a cat, they are not solitary hunters that will shun the company of other cats. As long as food is freely available, adult cats will happily co-exist even if they are not related. Female cats and kittens are much less territorial and will form bonds with each other, particularly if they are related. However, in a domestic situation with several adult cats, each needs to have its own personal space – even if this is only theirs exclusively at certain times of the day, with another cat claiming it at other times. Despite their apparent independence, if one cat in a household dies, the other will certainly show signs of missing its companion, eating less and demanding more attention from its owner.

Cats will only be people-friendly if they have been introduced to humans when they are kittens. Having a mother that accepts and enjoys human company is also a big influence on the kitten's future behaviour. The kitten needs to get to know people before it is seven weeks old – although it should not be handled until it is at least two weeks old. Generally the more people that the kitten can have contact with in this period, the more outgoing it will be – if it is only handled by one person it may form a bond only with them.

Cats groom themselves regularly, partly to keep their coat free from tangles and loose hairs, but also to spread oil from the skin to waterproof the coat. In hot weather they lick their coats regularly as the layer of saliva helps to keep them cool. They also spend a great deal of their time asleep – it is estimated that the average cat will sleep for up to eighteen hours a day.

Training

Although a cat cannot be trained as a dog would be, it is possible to encourage them to do good things, and discourage them from bad behaviour. This really needs to be established when the cat is quite young – older cats find it difficult to learn new tricks. Dogs can be trained because they live in a hierarchical society, so accepting an owner as a dominant member of the pack and acting to please them is in their nature. Cats are independent so they are not interested in pleasing the boss. They will respond to rewards and punishment, however, just as they would learn from pleasant and unpleasant consequences in the wild. You can train a cat to use a litter tray, to sit on command, and to miaow in response if you call its name by using food treats as a reward. Direct punishment will cause the cat to associate you with unpleasant things, which is bad for your mutual relationship, but there are indirect methods: using a water pistol to squirt a badly-behaving cat, or dropping a metal foil box filled with rattling dried beans to startle it, will soon discourage it from some habits. To stop it jumping up on worktops or scratching upholstery, temporarily cover the item in thick plastic or add strips of double-sided tape. Do not forget to provide an alternate scratching post, and somewhere it can climb, to encourage lasting changes in behaviour.

KEEPING YOUR CAT HEALTHY

CARING FOR YOUR CAT

T here is a range of things that you can do to keep your cat healthy, protecting it from infectious diseases and accident, providing a balanced diet and dealing with any signs of illness promptly. Some cats will need more attention than others, particularly very young or very old animals.

Indoors or Outdoors

In the wild cats obviously live outdoors, and many owners – particularly those of non-pedigree cats – feel that access to the outside world offers their pet the most natural way of life. They have room to exercise and hunt, access to fresh air and lots of exciting smells, opportunities for entertainment and mating. Outdoor living does have its disadvantages, however. The cat originally developed in the wide open spaces of Africa, not in the urban environment where so many of them live now. Outside the cat is in danger from traffic, other animals and natural hazards like open water or poisonous plants. Even if there is an apparently safe garden, there is no guarantee that the cat will stay there – particularly if it has not been neutered – and other animals can still come in, which may attack the resident cat, or transfer fleas or infectious diseases. The cat itself may also present a danger to local wildlife – and there may be local laws in place protecting wild birds or other wild animals.

Since the cat is adaptable, most will accept a totally indoor life and even be quite happy and contented. For some cats – such as the hairless Sphynx and cats that have been declawed – an indoor life is essential. The Sphynx and other breeds like it have little protection from cold or sun, so they need to be kept warm and sheltered. Declawed cats are unable to climb trees to escape attack or to defend themselves. An indoor cat will need entertainment to keep it happy and stimulated – battery-powered toys provide an acceptable substitute for prey and you can change the environment and give the cat something new to explore just by adding something like an upside down cardboard box. Cats like to climb, but you can encourage your indoor cat to climb in suitable places by providing a cosy space on top of an old piece of furniture, for instance. Provide a litter tray in an easily accessible place and make sure it is cleaned regularly, as cats will refuse to use one if it is inconvenient or too smelly. Check all indoor plants – cats chew grass outside, both to help digestion and for the fibrous sensation. Houseplants may seem like an acceptable substitute to the cat, but apart from the fact that you may not want your plants chewed, some are toxic. Check not only the label but also in a good plant book, and consider providing something specifically for the cat such as a pot of ordinary grass or a spider plant (*Chlorophytum comosum*).

Food

All creatures need a balanced diet to thrive, but a cat's needs are more fine-tuned than most. A cat is a carnivore, so it must have meat – some of the vital amino acids and fats it needs are found only in meat; a deficiency can lead to serious health problems, such as blindness and heart disease. A cat also needs particularly high levels of protein, but is prone to certain medical conditions if it has too much of some foods. The best way to ensure your cat has all the vitamins and minerals it needs is to feed a good-quality commercial cat food. There is no nutritional

Above: Establish a varied diet for your cat, or it will become too dependent on just one type of food.
Opposite: An overweight cat will need a special diet to help it slim down.

difference between the canned or dried type, but dried food will have less smell and can be left in the bowl all day. Be sure to throw away any leftover food daily and clean the bowl thoroughly. Cats fed on dried food also have fewer problems with their teeth, which may be due to the more abrasive nature of dried food. It is also cheaper than canned food. However, canned food is very palatable and more easily digested, so if your cat is unwell, underweight or off its food it can be a good choice. Feeding canned food regularly can lead to obesity, particularly in indoor cats – because it is so palatable it is easy for a cat to overeat, and indoor cats do not get enough exercise to counteract this. Canned food needs to be kept in the refrigerator after the can is open, and any unused food in the bowl must be thrown away quickly – it cannot be left out in case the cat fancies it later. Semi-moist food, as its name suggests, falls between dried and canned food. It has some of the advantages of both and falls between the two in price.

Whichever type of food you choose, it is important to establish a varied diet for your cat. If it becomes addicted to a certain food that is not nutritionally

complete and refuses alternatives, it can develop health problems. A particular food may also become unavailable for some reason, and a cat's digestion is very finely-tuned and reacts badly to sudden change. If you do have to change brands, try to do so gradually, mixing the new and old in ever changing portions, until you are one hundred per cent onto the new food. Whether to provide meals at fixed times or establish free-choice feeding is down to preference and to what kind of food you choose. Canned food cannot be left out, so needs to be provided at specific times. Both dry and semi-moist food can be left out all day for the cat to eat when it wishes, and many small meals instead of one big one is good for the cat's health. However, unlimited food all day can quickly lead to obesity, or you may not notice quickly if your cat is off its food. Perhaps the best option is to provide food for free-choice feeding, but for only a limited period each day.

Grooming

All cats will benefit from regular grooming – perhaps once a week – but some longhaired breeds need grooming once a day. Brushing and combing a cat will not only be soothing for both of you, it will also remove loose hair, which would otherwise end up on your furniture or be removed as the cat cleans itself and be coughed up as a hair ball. With outdoor cats, grooming will also give you a chance to check regularly for fleas. If you think your cat has a problem, comb its fur with a flea comb – flea debris looks like little black flecks, but if you drop them onto damp paper a red halo will form.

Left: A longhaired cat must be groomed regularly. If its fur becomes matted, professional grooming with an electric clipper may be the only answer.

Alternatively you can look for the fleas themselves by parting the cat's fur and looking close to the skin. Longhaired cats often need daily grooming to prevent their coats matting. Once the fur has formed a mat it is difficult to remove — large areas of matting must be removed with clippers by a professional. Some cats, such as the Cornish Rex, have coats that need special grooming, and it is best to check with the breeder how to proceed. Hairless breeds like the Sphynx do not require brushing, but wiping down with a chamois leather daily will remove excess oil from the skin.

Above: Kittens will play with anything in reach, but can be seriously injured if they bite through electric cables.
Opposite: Keep the doors of household appliances closed when inquisitive kittens are around.

Keeping kittens safe

Playing with your kitten is an important part of the bonding process, but kittens will also play quite happily on their own. Very young kittens have little sense of danger, so make sure that they cannot fall down steps, bump or fall into anything or knock heavy objects over. Never allow a kitten to play with anything they might swallow – such as rubber bands, yarn or lengths of ribbon. These can easily cause major health problems if they become twisted up inside the cat. Another favourite with young cats is playing with electric cables. They will pounce, particularly if the cable moves – on an iron while you are ironing, for instance. Not only will the kitten probably get a fatal electric shock if it bites through the cable, it may also pull the iron, or even something larger, down onto itself. Older cats will be less inclined to play with anything lying around on the floor.

HEALTH PROBLEMS

Most cats will be healthy most of the time, but there are various illnesses that crop up often in the feline population. Some breeds have hereditary health problems, so if buying a pedigree animal from a breeder, make sure it has a clean bill of health. Minor cuts and scratches picked up by outdoor cats will often heal themselves, but keep an eye on them and keep the cat indoors if possible, to avoid the risk of secondary infections. A range of non-serious common health problems plus a few more serious ones are covered here. General signs of illness include lethargy, change in appetite, change in grooming habits, weight loss, change in behaviour or changes in the way the cat uses the litter tray. Always take your cat to the vet if it appears to be unwell, and wash your hands carefully after handling a sick animal.

Common health problems

Eye problems are indicated by redness of the area around the eye, pawing or rubbing of the eyes, excessive tears or a discharge, a visible third eye or cloudiness or colour change in the eye. Causes include viral or bacterial infections, eyes that have been physically injured, allergies or congenital problems leading to tear duct overflow. Eye infections will spread quickly, and a vet may prescribe antibiotic or antiviral drops.

An ear problem is indicated by the cat scratching or shaking its head. The most usual cause is ear mites, which will need to be cleaned out by a vet initially, although he or she may show you how to do this in future. Mites sometimes spread to the skin causing red, itchy patches, which will also need treatment.

Skin problems are indicated by red and sometimes itchy skin, scabs, hair loss and flaking skin. There are a wide range of possible causes, including parasites,

Opposite: After ear mites have been cleaned away, the vet will administer ear drops.

infection, food or environmental allergies, or ringworm. It is difficult even for a vet to make an exact diagnosis, as symptoms may be the same for different causes, and may be different from cat to cat. Fleas are the easiest problem to treat at home, and although they may not sound serious a bad infestation can cause anaemia and the fleas can carry other diseases.

Bad breath is usually caused by gum infection, but this may be virus related. Check your cat's teeth regularly to see if there is build up of tartar. Occasional vomiting is possibly due to hair balls being regurgitated, but may also be related to diet or to eating grass. Serious vomiting indicates a deeper problem and should be checked out. Diet problems may also cause diarrhoea or constipation – a cat's digestive system is so finely tuned that it can even develop these if you simply change the brand of cat food you are providing.

Sneezing or coughing may just indicate an allergy, or something like a blade of grass in the nose – but they may equally indicate the onset of something more

Below: Routine worming will clear your cat of any internal parasites.

serious. If no other symptoms are present, just keep an eye on the animal. Breathing difficulties indicate a chest infection of some kind, or asthma, which is potentially fatal.

One common problem that often has few external signs is an infestation of internal parasites. These include roundworms, hookworms, tapeworms, coccidian, giardia and toxoplasmosis. With some of these the only sign that a cat is infected may be signs of the worm in its faeces or vomit, but some do not seem to affect the health of the cat at all, so they are difficult to spot. Routine examination and testing is the only reliable way to ensure your cat has not become infested – and it is important that the animal is treated as some of these parasites can infect humans. Toxoplasmosis is particularly dangerous to pregnant women, while roundworms can cause blindness in young children.

Most cats will have bladder or urinary tract infections at some point in their lives. Signs include frequent urination, sometimes stained with blood, and cats licking the genital area regularly and often to relieve the pain. Giving plenty of water to drink will help to prevent these infections, although the cause of them is not really known. If not treated, cats will recover but sometimes not for several weeks.

Obese cats are prone to heart problems and diabetes, but these can often be kept under control with medication. Some breeds are prone to congenital heart problems, such as the Siamese.

Serious health problems
There are several viral diseases that cats can suffer from. Feline leukaemia virus (FeLV) is spread from cat to cat through saliva, and can affect the cat in many ways. It may cause cancer, it may break down the immune system so the cat suffers a variety of secondary illnesses, or it may cause other problems like severe anaemia. Of all the viral illnesses that a cat might suffer, FeLV kills the most cats. There is a vaccine available, and all cats at risk should have it, but it does not always work and there is no cure. Indoor cats are less at risk as they are not exposed to other animals.

Cats can also catch a feline immunodeficiency virus (FIV) that acts in the same way as the human variety, HIV. An infected animal may have no symptoms at all at first, but gradually the immune system will break down and a host of

Above: Outdoor cats are in danger from traffic as well as other animals - this one has a broken leg.
Opposite: Cats will be happier going to the vet if their pet carrier is a familiar place with some of
their toys or a blanket inside.

secondary infections will become established which will eventually kill the animal. There is no cure, so try to keep your cat away from any infected animals.

Feline infectious peritonitis (FIP) sometimes develops as a result of a viral infection, but it is rare in domestic cats. However it is much less rare in places that have a large concentration of cats, such as breeding centres, so if you buy a cat from such a place you should make sure it is disease-free and vaccinated. The vaccine is effective, but if the cat gets the disease there is no cure.

Another highly contagious and deadly virus is feline panleukopenia, otherwise known as feline distemper or feline infectious enteritis. It is not particularly common, but again is more prevalent in catteries where there is a large population of cats in a small area. Adult cats may not show any symptoms, but kittens will either die or suffer brain damage.

Rabies also affects cats as well as dogs, but has not spread in either Great Britain or North America. All cats should be vaccinated against it, however, particularly if they may travel – in some countries the vaccination is obligatory.

Cancer can also affect cats in the same way as humans, with uncontrolled growth of cells that cannot be stopped by the body's natural immune system. The most common cancer in cats is lymphosarcoma, in which the lymph nodes are affected. It is caused by FeLV, so limiting your cat's interaction with other cats will cut down its chances of getting this form, which can be treated but is incurable. Other cancers can affect the skin, mouth and bones.

Caring for a sick cat

A seriously ill cat will be kept at the vet's and treated there, but you may have to continue treatment after the cat returns home. There are also less serious

Above: A sick cat needs to be kept warm and given plenty of fluids. This kitten has cat flu.

conditions that can be treated entirely at home. Many cats will hide away when they become ill, and they do not want to be fussed over. Provide somewhere warm for your cat to sleep and make sure that it takes food and water. Offer something easier to digest if it is off its food, or a special treat to tempt its appetite. If it is not drinking, make sure you give water with a syringe – just a little at a time – as dehydration is very dangerous. It may help to warm food and drink to body temperature.

If the cat needs medicines, follow the vet's instructions. Cats will not take whole pills inside food, nor will they readily eat food that has medicine sprinkled on it. The best way is to get the cat to swallow a pill by putting it at the back of the throat, but you may need both practice and help to do this. Eye drops and ear drops should also be given at blood temperature, so heat the bottle in your hands before you begin. If you then hold the cat's head gently and move quickly and decisively, you should have no problems administering such medicine. If a cat is totally uncooperative when you try to treat it, you can keep it still by wrapping its body in a towel, with only the head protruding, and holding it close against your body. It will be unable to lash out with its feet, but be careful that you do not get bitten.

First aid

If your cat is injured, try to keep calm and first block any escape routes, as its natural instinct will be to hide away. Approach the animal slowly and calmly and place a towel over its head, avoiding any sudden movements, to prevent it biting you. Examine any visible injuries and if possible stem any bleeding with pressure.

Check the cat is breathing – if not, see if the airway is obstructed by pulling the tongue forward and looking down the throat. You may be able to remove any problem with a sharp rap on the chest. You can perform artificial respiration by extending the cat's head, holding its mouth closed and blowing gently into the nostrils every three seconds. Check the heartbeat and if it has stopped you can compress the chest between thumb and forefinger to massage the heart. If there is no heartbeat or breathing after 20 minutes, the cat cannot be revived. If the cat has a heartbeat and is breathing unaided, keep it warm and still while you speak to a vet. To transport the cat to a vet, place it gently in a box or a top opening cat carrier, trying not to twist the spine in case it is injured.

If a cat has obviously broken a leg, do not try to splint the fracture but clean the area if possible and cover with a clean dressing until you can get to the vet. Wounds can also have a temporary dressing. Cats that are not obviously injured may suffer from shock. Signs include pale gums, a weak rapid pulse, rapid breathing and skin and legs cool to the touch. Keep the animal warm and take it to the vet straight away.

Older cats

If well cared for, cats can live for twenty years but an older cat may need more looking after than a younger one. As cats age, they may begin to display changes in the behaviour patterns that have been established over many years, and these changes are often caused by medical problems. A previously placid cat, for example, may become more aggressive because it is experiencing pain or because it can no longer hear or see properly and therefore feels threatened. Have older cats checked out regularly by the vet, as this may pick up any problems before they have a chance to develop. The senior citizen may need extra help with the litter tray and to groom itself. Make sure it is still taking adequate food and water – older cats may need more water than younger ones, due to the increased risk of kidney problems. If you feel your cat is suffering, consider euthanasia. It is hard to lose a beloved companion, but you should not keep a cat alive with a poor quality of life just to salve your own feelings. If your cat does die, allow yourself time to grieve properly.

Right: Older cats should have a routine check up every year to pick up health problems before they become too distressing.

PREGNANT CATS AND NEW-BORN KITTENS

I n general it is best to avoid allowing domestic cats to breed as there are already too many unwanted cats in the world. If your cat does become pregnant, she will need constant access to food – she will start to eat more right from the onset. Make sure she can also still access water easily when she becomes bulky towards the end of the pregnancy. For about two weeks before she is due to deliver keep her indoors, so she does not find an unsuitable place outside in which to give birth. Give her a comfortable box instead, placed somewhere

Opposite: The pregnant cat will receive all the vitamins and minerals she needs from a proper diet.
Above: Several males may mate with the same female, so litter mates may have different fathers.

warm and secluded. It should be large enough for her to be able to stretch out and move around, but not so big that kittens can move too far away. As the birth time comes near, the cat will visit the box frequently, rearranging the bedding to her liking, and at this point it is wise to confine her to the room – although make sure she has access to food, water and a litter tray. The kittens will be born one at a time, and there may be some delay between them. If the mother senses that there is too much human intervention, or if something else disturbs her, she may stop delivering more kittens until the following day. The mother chews off the placenta and may eat it, as well as cleaning the kitten. There are usually around five kittens in a litter.

Above: A kitten at one day old. The kitten is blind at birth but its eyes will open after about a week.

There is no need for human intervention in this process unless the contractions proceed for more than an hour with no kitten being delivered, if a kitten only delivers partway and then appears to stick, or if the mother is lethargic or ill after delivery. If a kitten is rejected by the mother or appears to be still-born, it may be abnormal. Pick it up in a clean warm towel, and remove the membrane. If the placenta is still attached, tie it off with a piece of cotton about half an inch from the body, then cut the placenta further down. If the kitten is not breathing you can clean the mouth with a sterile cloth and try to clear fluid from the lungs by holding it carefully in one or both cupped hands and swinging your arms downward in an arc a few times. Massage the body to stimulate breathing. If you manage to resuscitate the kitten, see if its mother will accept it – if not, you can try hand rearing but it may not survive.

Above: A kitten at five weeks. Before four weeks they should not be handled too much but after eight weeks they will not be receptive to human company if they are not used to it.

A few days after giving birth the mother will move her kittens to a different location, as to her mind the birth place is dangerous because the smell may attract predators. Make sure she has plenty of water and food while she is feeding the kittens, which will be for the first month of their life. After this the kittens can start taking a specially formulated kitten food.

Kittens

Newborn kittens weigh around 100g (4oz) but they will double their birth weight within seven days. They will suckle up to three times an hour, so as the mother will need to provide plenty of milk, she needs plenty of food herself. If she does not provide sufficient milk for all the kittens, they will cry constantly and fail to stay at the nipple. Supplementing their diet with a commercial feline formula will be essential, or they will die. Cat milk is very rich in fat and protein, so cows' milk, goats' milk or baby formula is not a suitable substitute. By 21 days the kittens will have trebled in weight – and males may grow even faster. The kittens continue to suckle for up to six weeks, but by three weeks they are ready to try some solid food and by eight weeks they should be fully weaned. In the wild, the mother brings prey back to the nest for the kittens to eat – first tearing it up for them, then leaving them to do more of the work. Finally the mother brings live prey for the kittens to catch and kill themselves.

At birth the kitten is blind, deaf and is unable to regulate its body temperature so the room around the nesting box should be at a constant temperature of 32–34°C (90–94°F). Within a few days the young will be able to find its mother and within a week it will recognize the smell of the nest and will return if it becomes separated. By two weeks its eyes and ears will have begun to open. Within three weeks the kitten can also stand on four legs, see and respond and by seven weeks it will be running around. Steady weight gain and a good appetite are signs that things are going well. The kitten should be checked out by the vet and given its first vaccinations when it is around six to eight weeks old. It should certainly be vaccinated before it leaves the litter for a new home, which can be as early as eight to nine weeks. Breeders of pedigree cats will usually prefer to wait for longer to see if the kitten will be a suitable show cat.

Right: A kitten at nine weeks. By this time it should be fully weaned, been checked by the vet and have had its first vaccinations.

The mother's licking of her kittens not only cleans them but also stimulates them to urinate and defecate. By three weeks the kitten has learned to control these functions and may begin to use a litter tray. The cat's urge to use a specific site is inbuilt – it is part of its naturally hygienic nature. Clumping litter is not ideal for kittens, as they may confuse it with dried food.

Kittens learn to hunt from their mother, but can also learn other skills – such as how to open latches! The receptive learning period of a cat is quite short, however, so if they are to spend their lives in human company, kittens need to start socializing with people as soon as possible. The critical period is between four and eight weeks – before four weeks they should not be handled too much, but after eight weeks they will not be receptive to human company if they are not used to it. If the cat is to live with a family it should also be accustomed to children at this time or it will not be able to form a bond with them later. In the wild, the males will be expelled from the nest by around six months and the females will stay to form a continuing social group.

Left: Cats carry their kittens by the scruff of the neck, which triggers a reflex action in the kitten, causing it to curl up and tuck its legs away to avoid them being damaged.

DEALING
WITH BEHAVIOURAL
PROBLEMS

C ats very rarely exhibit true psychotic behaviour – the problem is that they may behave in ways that are natural to them, but which we find annoying or offensive. Some of these problems can easily be tackled by studying cats' behaviour in the wild, and then using some common sense strategies to adapt these to their domestic life. Be careful not to shout at your pet or physically discipline it – this kind of behaviour will soon teach your companion that you are a source of unpleasant experiences, which is not good for your ongoing relationship. You need to apply discipline from a distance, so the animal learns to associate the unpleasant consequence with its own actions – not with your presence.

Refusing to use the litter tray

Cats are naturally hygienic animals that do not usually soil the area they live in, so if an animal refuses to use the litter tray and takes its business elsewhere there is usually a good reason. It is just a matter of establishing what that may be. Is the litter tray smelly – has it been cleaned regularly enough? Cats do not like to use a dirty litter tray. Is the litter tray sited in a bad spot? Like humans, most cats prefer a bit of privacy, so if the tray is near areas of noisy household traffic or in a cold draughty spot, move it to somewhere more amenable. Does your cat object to the litter granules you are using? If the animal is new to your household you may need

Opposite: If your cat has litter box lapses there may be several causes.
A covered litter box may help as it offers the cat some privacy.

Above: Buying or making a scratching post and encouraging your cat to use it will help to stop it spoiling the furniture.

to try a few brands until you find one that it prefers. Cats are very sensitive to smell and to the feel of the litter and changes that may seem unimportant to you can make a big difference to a cat. If litter lapses are occurring in a cat that was previously fine, consider if ill health may be the cause. If the cat is suffering from cystitis or blocked anal sacs it will soon associate the pain of these with the litter tray and will try going elsewhere.

MARKING TERRITORY

Scent marking

Do not confuse problems with the litter tray with scent marking. When cats mark their territory with urine they do not squat as normal but back up to a vertical surface, raise the tail and eject a spray of urine onto it. The smell is intended as a marker to show other cats that the territory is occupied, but it is offensive to humans and very difficult to get rid of. A neutered cat will rarely urine-mark, but only if this is done before the behaviour becomes established. Otherwise you can try to cut down this activity by spraying the cat with a short burst from a water pistol just as it takes aim. After some persistence, the cat will associate the cold water with unwanted behaviour and it should diminish.

Scratching

Scratching trees at a visible level is another way that a cat signals to other cats that it is in residence. When this behaviour is transferred to the legs of the best dining table, it is extremely annoying for the owner. The problem needs to be tackled in two ways. First, make sure that the cat has a scratching post to use as a substitute, which – initially at least – should be placed in a prominent position in the room. From the cat's point of view, it is no good marking something that cannot be seen! As the cat becomes used to using it, it can be gradually moved to a less obvious place as long as it is still in sight. Secondly, again either arm yourself with a water pistol and spray the cat with cold water as it begins to scratch, or be ready with something noisy such as a tin box filled with dried beans that you can drop to startle the animal. After a while the cat will learn that its scratching has unpleasant consequences.

Eating problems

If a cat is refusing to eat, make sure first that there is no underlying health problem. Being off its food is an early warning sign for many common illnesses, so it is worth getting the vet to check everything out. Once illness has been ruled out as a cause, you can look for other reasons. Again, consider the position of the feeding bowl – is it placed conveniently for you, or conveniently for your cat? It should be in a quiet area, free from draughts and through-traffic. Is the cat being disturbed as it eats? Make sure small children leave it alone at this time, and if you have other pets make sure they are not interrupting the feeding routine. If you have more than one cat, each should have its own bowl. Check the bowl itself – it should be thoroughly cleaned regularly; plastic bowls particularly have a tendency to take in unpleasant odours after a period of use. Cats are sensitive to nasty smells and will not eat from a smelly bowl. Finally, remember that cats can be just like children – do not allow feeding time to become a battle of wills. The cat can go without food for some time if it has to, and it is all too easy for the owner to give in and offer tasty treats – which will soon teach the cat that refusing to eat brings rich rewards.

Aggression

Cats are born to hunt, so if an animal cannot hunt for itself its natural aggression will need to find other outlets. This may turn out to be pouncing on an owner's ankles as they walk, which can be both unpleasant and painful. Give your cat alternative toys, and again you could press the water gun into action to discourage unwanted behaviour. Kittens try out their hunting instincts when they play, pouncing and biting at anything that moves. This may be cute but when playing with a kitten do not encourage nipping of your hands or other similar behaviour, as this is only teaching it that biting humans is acceptable. A nip from a kitten can soon turn into a nasty bite from an adult cat. Some cats suddenly lash out as they are being petted or stroked. Possibly the animal has just had enough, or in a male its instinct to keep away from rival animals may have kicked in. If this kind of behaviour occurs regularly with your pet, try to restrict your stroking to short periods of time.

Jumping and climbing

Jumping and climbing are a natural part of the cat's behaviour, but jumping up on kitchen worktops is unhygienic and there may be other surfaces you want the cat to avoid – such as a baby's bed or changing table. Tackle such problems as soon as you can, as if behaviour becomes established it is much harder to eradicate later. Again the water gun can be used, but this depends on your constant presence to

Opposite: Jumping and climbing is a natural part of the cat's behaviour, but it can be discouraged from jumping up where it is not wanted.

catch the culprit in the act. Try covering hard surfaces temporarily with tinfoil, or with strips of double-sided tape (on sheets of paper or cardboard if it cannot be put directly on the surface). The cat will not like the feel of these materials under its feet, so will tend to go somewhere else. Another possibility is to startle the animal with a 'booby trap' — obviously something that will not hurt it, but teach it to associate an unpleasant experience with being in that spot. A false cardboard edge on a shelf can be rigged so it falls when the cat jumps on it, possibly also bringing down something light but noisy, such as tinfoil cartons. Remember to designate one area where the cat can climb or jump as an alternative.

Plant eating

Cats often eat grass — it is an aid to their digestion and they like the fibrous texture. Cats indoors may begin chewing your favourite houseplants instead. Provide an alternative, such as a spider plant (*Chlorophytum comosum*) or a pot of ordinary grass. Discourage the cat from chewing the houseplant by moving it to somewhere less accessible, or by spraying it with anti-chew spray, available from pet shops.

Left: Cats eat grass both to aid their digestive processes and because they like the texture. Beware of poisonous plants in both the garden and the home, including Ivy (Hedera), Asparagus Fern (Asparagus densiflorus), Poinsettia (Euphorbia pulcherrima) and Sweetheart Plant (Philodendron species).

GLOSSARY

Agouti hairs – the pale hairs in a tabby coat, with bands of light and dark colour ending in a dark tip. Also used to refer to the pale parts of the tabby coat.

Awn hairs – bristly intermediate hair, longer than the down hair but shorter than the guard hair, which help with insulation and protect the down hair. See also down hair and guard hair.

Backcross – to breed a cat back to one of its parents.

Bicolour – a white coat with patches of another colour on back, tail and head.

Boots – white paws on the hindlegs of a coloured or bi-coloured cat. Also called gauntlets.

Breeches – longer thicker hair on the back of a cat's upper hindlegs.

Breed – cats with the same physical characteristics, descended from the same ancestors. Usually produced by human intervention.

Breed Standard – a description of the ideal features against which each cat in a breed is measured.

Britches – US term for breeches.

Burmese pattern – coat with the darkest colour on the head, limbs and tail, with the body a slightly paler shade of the same colour.

Calico – a coat pattern of white with large patches of red and black, or cream and blue. Like the Tortoiseshell, a Calico is almost certainly female.

Castrate – to neuter a male cat by removing the testicles.

Cattery – an establishment breeding cats.

Chinchilla – a longhair cat with a ticked coat pattern in which the hairs are light or white except for a tip of darker colour at the ends; or this type of coat in any cat.

Classic tabby – a tabby coat with large swirling stripes on back and legs and blotches on the flanks.

Cobby – a body type that is short, broad and heavy-boned.

Colourpoint – a pointed coat pattern, in which the face, ears, tail and legs are a solid colour darker than the body colour.

Dander – scales of dead skin, which can cause an allergic reaction in humans.

Deep colour – the rich self or solid coat colour, usually black or red, seen when the colour is distributed evenly along the length of the hair.

Dilute colour – less saturated coat colour, such as blue or cream, seen when the colour is unevenly distributed along the length of the hair.

Domestic shorthair – an ordinary housecat, or non-purebred cat.

Dominant gene – a gene carrying a trait that is always expressed.

Double coat – a coat in which the undercoat is thick and dense and which also has a thick topcoat.

Down hairs – soft insulating secondary hairs in the undercoat. See also awn hair and guard hair.

Estrous – female reproductive cycle. US spelling of Oestrous.

Estrus – phase of the female cat's cycle when she is fertile (commonly called 'heat'). US spelling of Oestrus.

Euthanasia – use of medical means, usually a lethal injection, to cause death. Used to avoid suffering in sick and ageing pets, and to limit populations in cat shelters.

Feral cat – a descendant of a domestic cat living in the wild.

Free-breeding – animals choosing their own mates, without human intervention. Also called random breeding.

Frown lines – dark lines forming an M on a cat's forehead.

Gauntlets – white paws on the hindlegs of a coloured or bi-coloured cat. Also called boots.

Gene pool – collection of all genes, both dominant and recessive, available in any one species, race or breed.

Ghost markings – faint tabby markings sometimes seen in the coat of non-agouti cats, or in kittens, they often fade with age.

Gloves – white forepaws on a coloured or bi-coloured cat, usually stopping below the ankle. Also called mittens.

Guard hairs – coarse, thick, protective hairs that protect the undercoat and provide a waterproof topcoat. See also awn hair and down hair.

Hock – back leg joint, the cat's ankle.

Inbreeding – mating of related cats.

Kitten – a young cat still dependent on its mother; commonly used for those older than this but not fully grown.

Kitten cap – white cats carry a dominant gene that masks other colours, but kittens sometimes show a hint of their underlying colour on their heads, which vanishes with age.

Locket – a small patch of white hair on the chest of a coloured cat, often seen as a fault in pedigree cats.

Lynx point – US term for a pointed coat in which the points have underlying tabby stripes, otherwise known as Tabby point.

Mackerel tabby – tabby coat pattern with vertical stripes running from the spine like the bones of a fish skeleton.

Manx – breed of cat without a tail, caused by a mutated gene.

Mascara lines – dark lines extending from the outer corners of the eye.

Mink – a coloured body with moderate pointing, the characteristic pattern of the Tonkinese breed, a combination of the pointed and sepia patterns. See also pointed, sepia.

Mitted – coat pattern marked with white on the paws, chin, chest, belly and back legs.

Mittens – white forepaws on a coloured or bi-coloured cat, usually stopping below the ankle. Also called gloves.

Mosaicing – random patching or mottled coat colours, such as the tortoiseshell.

Mutation – a genetic accident that changes certain genetic characteristics.

Neuter – render incapable of breeding by surgically removing the reproductive organs. Known as castrating in male and spaying in female cats.

Nictitating membrane – a thin protective membrane located at the inner corner of the eye (sometimes called the 'third eyelid'), which draws across the eye if the cat is sick or injured.

Non-agouti hairs – one-colour, non-banded hairs that make up self or solid-colour coats, or the dark areas in a tabby coat.

Odd-eyes – cat with two different coloured eyes.

Oestrous – female reproductive cycle. Spelt estrous in the US.

Oestrus – phase of the female cat's cycle when she is fertile (commonly called 'heat'). Spelt estrus in the US.

Oriental type – a body type that is tubular, long-legged and fine-boned.

Outcross – to breed a cat with another of a different breed, in order to strengthen the stock, refine and build features, and increase colour variations.

Patched tabby – a cat with a tortoiseshell coat pattern that is also marked by one of the four tabby patterns. Known in the US as a Torbie.

Pedigree – the line of parentage in purebred cats, through several generations, a certificate of unmixed breeding.

Piebald – a coat pattern featuring white with any other colour or pattern.

Pointed – a coat pattern with a light-coloured torso marked with darker shades at the body's extremities, the ears, muzzle, paws and tail, which was first known in the Siamese breed. See also mink, sepia, colourpoint, tabby point and tortie point.

Polydactyl – a genetic mutation that causes extra toes on a cat's paws.

Purebred – a cat descended from unmixed parentage within a single recognized breed.

Random breeding – animals choosing their own mates, without human intervention. Also called free-breeding.

Recessive gene – a genetic trait that can be carried without being expressed.

Registry – a recognized organization keeping a record of purebred cats.

Rex – a term for any mutation causing a curly coat. The coat has no guard hairs but a soft, curly undercoat.

Ruff – a collar of longer fur around the neck.

Scent marking – traces of urine or scent from glands, left by cats to mark their territory or signal their presence in the breeding season. Occasionally used to signal stress in the household (such as overcrowding). Sometimes known as urine marking.

Selective breeding – breeding in which the partners are determined with human intervention.

Self – a coat in one colour, formed of non-agouti hairs. Also called Solid.

Sepia – coat pattern in which the darkest colour is restricted to the head, limbs and tail, with the body a slightly paler shade of the same colour. See also mink, pointed.

Shaded – a ticked coat pattern in which the hair is lighter or white at the base, extending to about half the length of the hair, and the top half of the hair is darker. See also silvering, smoke, tipped.

Siamese pattern – a light-coloured torso marked with darker shades at the body's extremities, the ears, muzzle, paws and tail. See also pointed.

Silvering – a coat in which the yellow tint has been suppressed, leaving part of the hair very pale or white and giving the cat a silvery appearance. See also shading, smoke, tipped.

Single coat – a coat in which the undercoat is missing or is very thin.

Smoke a self or solid coat in which just the base of the hair is light or white. See also shaded, silvering, tipped.

Socialization – the process by which a cat becomes used to the presence of humans and other animals.

Solid – a coat in one colour, formed of non-agouti hairs. Also called self.

Spay – to sterilize a female cat by removing the ovaries and most of the uterus.

Spectacles – areas of lighter fur around the eyes, particularly below.

Spotted tabby – a tabby coat pattern with dark blotches or spots against a background of agouti hairs.

Tabby – any of the variety of coat patterns produced by a combination of agouti hairs (in the pale areas) and non-agouti hairs (in the darker stripes or spots). There are four traditional patterns: classic, mackerel, spotted and ticked.

Tabby point – a pointed coat in which the points have underlying tabby stripes, known in the US as Lynx point.

Third eyelid – a thin protective membrane located at the inner corner of the eye (the nictitating membrane) which draws across the eye if the cat is sick or injured.

Ticked tabby – a tabby coat pattern in which the entire coat features banded agouti hairs.

Ticking – banding of light and dark colours along a hair.

Tipped – coat of white hairs with coloured tips. See also shaded, silvering, smoke.

Tonkinese pattern – a coloured body with moderate pointing, the characteristic pattern of the Tonkinese breed, a combination of the pointed and sepia patterns.

Topcoat – the cat's protective coat of coarse guard hairs, which also carries the pattern in tabbies. Also called the outer coat.

Torbie – the US term for a patched tabby.

Tortie point – a type of pointed coat pattern in which the points have an underlying tortoiseshell pattern.

Tortoiseshell – a coat pattern typically in both black and red fur in deep coats, or blue and cream in dilute coats.

Undercoat – the part of a cat's coat beneath the topcoat. See also Awn hairs, Down hairs.

Urine marking – traces of urine left by cats to mark their territory, or signal their presence in the breeding season. Occasionally used to signal stress in the household (such as overcrowding). Sometimes known as scent marking.

Van – a piebald-type cat pattern in which most of the body is white, with small patches of colour mainly on the head and tail.

BREED
REGISTRIES

BREED REGISTRIES

GREAT BRITAIN

Governing Council of the Cat Fancy (GCCF)

4-6 Penel Orlieu, Bridgwater,

Somerset, TA6 3PG. UK

Tel: +44 (0)1278 427 575

E-mail: info@gccfcats.org

Website: http://ourworld.compuserve.com/homepages/GCCF_CATS

Formed in 1910, the GCCF keeps registers, licenses and controls cat shows, looks after the welfare of pedigree cats and ensures that the rules set up are not broken. It registers around 32,000 cats.

EUROPE

Fédération Internationale Féline (FIFe)

Website: www.fifeweb.org

A European federation representing organizations in forty countries, all using the same breed standards and rules.

UNITED STATES

American Association of Cat Enthusiasts (AACE)

PO Box 213, Pine Brook, NJ 07058. USA

Tel: +1 (973) 335-6717

Fax: +1 (973) 334-5834

Email: info@aaceinc.org

Website: www.aaceinc.org

Founded in 1993, AACE aims to give exhibitors rewarding and fun Cat Shows, to give the exhibitor a fair appraisal of their cat, while making sure that the judge is treated fairly and is not under pressure to follow any political groups directions, and to keep the cat the number one priority. AACE recognizes 47 breeds in the Championship/Alter classes, and has a Household Pet class. Since 1993 AACE has registered over 10,000 cats, 1,000 catteries, and has 25 member clubs.

American Cat Fanciers Association (ACFA)

P.O. Box 1949, Nixa, MO 65714-1949, USA

Tel: +1 (417) 725-1530

ax: + 1 (417) 725-1533

E-mail: acfa@aol.com

Website: www.acfacats

The American Cat Fanciers Association was formed in 1955 by a group of Cat Fanciers seeking greater flexibility in the development of cats, the activities of cat lovers and greater freedom for growth and harmony with contemporary needs of the individual breeders and the broadening horizons of the Cat Fancy at large.

The Cat Fanciers' Association (CFA)

P.O. Box 1005, Manasquan, NJ 08736-0805, USA

Tel: +1 (732) 528-9797 Fax: +1 (732) 528-7391

Website: www.cfainc.org

The Cat Fanciers' Association is a non-profit organization that was founded in 1906. The first cat shows licensed by CFA were held during 1906 - one in Buffalo and one in Detroit. The first Annual Meeting was held in 1907 at Madison Square Garden. In 1909, CFA published the first Stud Book and Register in both the Cat Journal magazine and as a book. CFA shows are judged using CFA breed standards.

Cat Fanciers' Federation (CFF)

P.O. Box 661, Gratis, OH 45330, USA

Tel: +1 (937) 787-9009 Fax: +1 (937) 787-4290

E-mail cff@siscom.net Website: www.cffinc.org

The Cat Fanciers' Federation (CFF) originated in 1919, chartered as a non-profit corporation based in Connecticut. In 1972, the Connecticut Corporation was dissolved and the Corporation was reorganized in Rhode Island. The first Studbook and register was published in 1922. The CFF registers pedigreed cats, household pets and catteries, licenses cat shows, maintains and updates standards for each feline breed, and looks after the health and welfare of all cats.

The International Cat Association (TICA)

Executive Office, P.O. Box 2684, Harlingen, TX 78551, USA

Tel: +1 (956) 428-8046 Fax: +1 (956) 428-8047

Website: www.tica.org

TICA was formed in 1979, by a group of several former ACFA members. It registers breeds according to genetic makeup, but cat shows are judged on the animal's appearance.

National Cat Fancier Association (NCFA)

10215 W. Mt., Morris Road, Flushing, MI 48433, USA

Tel: +1 (810) 659-9517

E-mail: cattie@Ameritech.net

Traditional and Classic Cat International (TCCI)

7615 Clyde Way, Smartsville, CA 95977, USA

Website: www.tcainc.org

TCCI is a non-profit organization founded by a group of Siamese breeders and fanciers who favoured the old-style apple-head Siamese look, were dissatisfied with the extreme changes in the contemporary breed, and concerned about the related health issues. To date, TCCI has approved breed standards for 16 different cat breeds.

The Traditional Cat Association (TCA)

PO Box 178, Heisson, WA 98622-0178, USA

Website: www.traditionalcats.com

E-mail: info@traditionalcats.com

TCA is a leading force behind the push to bring back the 'Original', 'Old Style' Traditional Siamese and Classic Siamese. TCA has over 30 breed standards and works to preserve and protect other Traditional Cats from near extinction.

United Feline Organization (UFO)

218 NW 180th Street, Newberry, FL. 32669, USA

Tel: +1 (352) 472-4701

E-mail: UFOIFL@att.net

UFO was founded in 1994 and accepts 60 breeds. It holds shows in the US, Canada, Japan and Mexico.

CANADA

Canadian Cat Association/Association Feline Canadienne (CCA)

289 Rutherford Road Suite 18

Brampton, Ontario, L6W 3R9, Canada

Tel: +1 (905) 459-1481 Fax: + 1 (905) 459-4023

E-mail: office@cca-afc.com Website: www.cca-afc.com

The CCA was founded in 1960, as a Canadian registry for purebred felines. Before this, all registrations had to be filed in the United States or Europe and all cat shows held in Canada were held under the rules of American associations. In 1961 registrations were entered in a Canadian stud book for the first time. The CCA promotes the welfare of all cats in Canada, looks to improve all breeds of cats in Canada and maintains a registry of purebred cats with over 190,000 individual cats registered.

AUSTRALIA

Australian Cat Federation (ACF)

P O Box 331, Port Adelaide BC, SA 5015, Australia

Tel: + 61 (08) 8449 5880

E-mail acfinc@chariot.net.au Website: www.acf.asn.au

The ACF was formed in 1972 and covers the whole of Australia with affiliates in all States and the Northern Territory. It promotes the welfare of all cats, the responsible breeding and showing of recognized breeds and the showing of domestic cats.

Feline Control Council of Victoria (FCCV)

1st Floor, 196 Bayswater Rd, Bayswater, Nth Victoria 3153, Australia

Tel: +61 (03) 9720 8811 Fax + 61 (03) 9729 6148

Email: fccvic@hotkey.net.au Website: www.hotkey.net.au/~fccvic

The FCCV was founded in 1962 to promote the welfare of cats, the general improvement of the standard, breeding and exhibition of cats, plus good sportsmanship among its members. It is the largest feline registration council in Victoria with approximately 900 members and recognized standards for 28 breeds of pedigreed cats.

INDEX

Acknowledgments

The publisher would like to thank Ardea.com, Animals Unlimited and NHPA for kindly providing the photographs in this book. We would also like to thank the following photographers for their kind permission to reproduce their photographs:

Ardea.com
Ardea London 10, 18,188; Yann Arthus-Bertrand 43t, 90,156,174,176; Brian Bevan 7,200,233; John Daniels: 1 ,4, 6,8, 13,14, 27,28, 33, 39,43b, 44, 46, 47, 48,49,50,52,55,56,60,62t, 64, 66, 72, 74, 76, 80, 84, 92, 94, 100, 103t&b, 118, 122, 128, 130, 132, 134, 138, 142, 144, 146, 148, 150, 172, 186, 192, 193, 194, 197, 198, 204, 205, 208, 211, 214, 215 ,216, 218, 220, 222, 223, 224, 228, 236, 240,251; Clem Haanger 22; Jean Michel Labat 2, 30, 31,32, 34,35,36, 38, 39,40,54, 58, 62b, 63, 68, 70,78, 86, 88, 96, 98,102, 104,106, 107,108,110, 112, 120, 124, 126, 140, 152, 160, 162, 170, 178, 191, 202, 209, 212, 221, 226, 230, 234, 239, 242,246; Tom & Pat Leeson 24; Johan de Meester 16, 154, 206; M. Watson 21

Animals Unlimited/Paddy Cutts:
82, 114, 116, 136, 158,164, 166, 167, 168

Yves Lanceau (NHPA):
180, 182, 184

Thank you to Sophie Napier and Angela Blackwood-Murray at Ardea, Tim Harris at NHPA and Paddy Cutts at Animals Unlimited for their invaluable help in producing this book.